Corvette
C3
1968–1982
Buyer's Guide

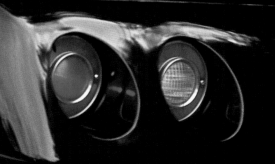

New Jersey · 11
NCRS 1
· Garden State ·

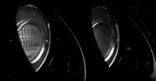

Richard Prince

MOTORBOOKS

First published in 2003 by Motorbooks, an imprint of MBI Publishing Company LLC, Galtier Plaza, Suite 200, 380 Jackson Street, St. Paul, MN 55101 USA.

MBI Publishing Company titles are also available at discounts in bulk quantity for industrial or sales-promotional use. For details write to Special Sales Manager at MBI Publishing Company, Galtier Plaza, Suite 200, 380 Jackson Street, St. Paul, MN 55101 USA.

ISBN-13: 978-0-7603-1655-9
ISBN-10: 0-7603-1655-4

Front Cover: 1969 Corvette C3

Frontispiece: Aluminum wheels were supposed to be optional in 1973, but porosity problems reportedly led to their cancellation. According to published production figures, only four cars were built with them before the option was discontinued. All remaining 1973s came with standard center caps and trim rings on rally rims, or with optional PO2 Deluxe Wheel Covers.

Title Page: Even though power was relatively low, 1977s were still quick cars by the standards of their day. Four-wheel disc brakes and a competent chassis enable them to stop and handle, too.

Edited by Chad Caruthers
Designed by Stephanie Michaud
Printed in Hong Kong

Richard Prince has owned, restored, raced, and enjoyed dozens of different Corvettes over the past 30 years. A writer and photographer for editorial, advertising, and corporate clients worldwide, his work and personal interests involve a wide variety of cars, though Corvettes occupy a special place in his heart. He lives in New York.

Contents

Dedicated to the memory of my grandparents. They were always there for me, and their love still influences all that I do.

Acknowledgments

A number of people very graciously assisted in the production of this book. Thank you to Ken and Patt Brown, Lewis Brown, Vito and Natalie Cimilluca, Richard Crump, Jack DiMaggio, Larry Harkavy, Bill Hermanek, John Kohronas, Gary Licko, Bill Mayes, Bill McBrien, Arthur Nastre, Mark Renz, Carlos Rivera, Stan Rivera, Dominick Salvemini and the crew at Vette Dreams, Bob Scorsone, Jason Scorsone, Alan Lauricella and the crew at Unique Corvettes, Bruce Silber, Ken Silber, Terry Strassberg, Corvette Mike Vietro, Dave Walters, John Waluk, Pam Waluk, and Dr. Otho Whiteneck. Thank you also to Chad Caruthers and Zack Miller for their patience and understanding. Finally, thank you to my sister Jamie, who has been a tremendous help, and to my wife, Carolyn, who is at my side every step of the way.

Introduction

When the first Corvette rolled off the assembly line some 50 years ago, few could have imagined where the marque would wind up. By virtue of unique, on-the-edge styling in concert with outstanding performance, the Corvette went from a curious anomaly in GM's vast arsenal to a sports car recognized and respected the world over.

Despite the fact that each successive generation of Corvette is vastly better than its predecessor, enthusiasm for vintage examples continues to increase. This is particularly true with regard to third-generation cars, known to collectors as C3s. Produced from 1968 through 1982, the C3 collection is the longest-lived model in Corvette history. Over the course of the C3's 15-year life span, some 542,861 C3s were built, a truly remarkable number for a relatively high-priced, high-performance sports car. The C3's production figures are equally remarkable when you consider what was happening in the automotive industry during that era.

The period between 1968 and 1982 was a fascinating and tumultuous time for automobiles. The beginning of this stretch marked the end of the golden era of Detroit muscle machines. Appropriately equipped Corvettes, such as those sporting the potent L88 or exotic ZL1 option packages, were the undisputed kings of the musclecar epoch.

As the 1960s turned into the 1970s, unrestrained power and speed fell victim to increasingly stringent insurance industry demands and governmental regulations, as well as new market considerations. Research and development dollars that had previously been directed toward enhancing performance were now targeted at meeting fuel economy, exhaust emissions, and safety requirements. As a result, all cars, including Corvettes, became heavier, clumsy looking, more expensive, and slower. The Corvette, however, weathered the storm with dignity and emerged from this rather gloomy era with its character and status intact.

As the 1970s came to a close, a transformation in the automobile-building business began to emerge. Technology had finally caught up with the mandates from the federal government and in fact was on the brink of surging ahead. Through the application of sophisticated computer technology, superior manufacturing techniques and materials, and high-tech electronics, Corvettes met all of the safety, emissions, and economy demands and performed admirably.

In the almost two decades since C3 production came to an end, collector interest in third-generation Corvettes has grown steadily. The sheer number of cars produced and the great variety of offerings during the Stingray's 15-year model run — including incredibly high-horsepower big blocks, efficient and powerful computer-directed small blocks, convertibles, and special offerings such as the 1978 Indy 500 Pace Car replica and 1982 Collector Edition—mean there is something of interest for just about everyone.

As is true of the collector-car hobby in general, purchasing a vintage Corvette is fraught with potential perils. Corvettes understandably tend to be driven with above-average enthusiasm and, not surprisingly, suffer collision damage at an above-average rate. Probably because fiberglass is relatively easy to work with, at least when compared to metal bodies, an inordinate number of unqualified people try their hand at fixing crashed Corvettes. The result is a large number of poorly repaired cars. Therefore, it is important to familiarize yourself with the telltale signs of collision damage and develop an understanding of correct and incorrect repair materials and techniques.

Besides the usual signs of previous body damage—poor panel fit; unacceptably wide, narrow, or irregular gaps between adjacent areas; and distorted understructures—you should also be on the lookout for inconsistencies in the body's factory-bonding arrangement. Corvette bodies were made from about two dozen separate panels that were glued together using bonding adhesive and bonding strips. Bonding strips are thin sections of fiberglass glued to the reverse sides of abutting panels. By recognizing what the reverse side of factory body panels, factory bonding strips, and factory bonding adhesives should look like, you can almost always spot replaced panels and repaired areas.

Though their fiberglass bodies are virtually immune to corrosion, the same is not true for the remainder of a Corvette. The body's underlying steel structure is prone to rust, especially in the framework surrounding the windshield, radiator support, and front body and bumper-support structures. The chassis is also vulnerable, most notably in the boxed side rails in the areas beneath and behind the doors.

Though mechanically stout, there are a few areas where time and high mileage tend to take a particularly harsh toll on C3 Corvettes. The independent rear suspension relies on a double rear-wheel bearing arrangement, and since there is no easy way to grease the bearings, they are often neglected and thus susceptible to failure beyond the 50,000-mile mark.

All C3s utilize the same four-wheel disc brake system which was first introduced in 1965. This system works extraordinarily well for stopping the car, but the caliper bores are susceptible to corrosion, owing to an electrolytic reaction that occurs between the aluminum pistons and their iron bores. Once the calipers corrode, they begin to leak fluid. New seals usually alleviate the leaks for a little while, but they don't solve the underlying problem, thus the leaks always return. The only long-term solution is to sleeve the caliper bores, preferably with stainless steel, and then install all new internal parts.

Despite these weaknesses, C3 Corvettes are inherently well-engineered and durable cars. They are also enjoyable to own and drive, excellent investments, and extremely well supported by the performance aftermarket and restoration-parts industries. Their over-the-road prowess is equal or superior to any other car of the era, and their beautiful, unique styling is every bit as exciting today as it was decades ago.

This buyer's guide provides background information and points out all of the important things to look for and look out for when contemplating the purchase of a C3. It is my sincere hope that you enjoy reading it as much as I've enjoyed writing it and it enhances the pleasure you derive from your participation in the vintage-Corvette hobby.

First-year new models have long had a reputation for being problematic, and 1968 Corvettes are no exception. Even so, a well-cared-for or nicely restored 1968 is a far better car than a neglected or poorly restored newer C3.

Corvette's transformation into a cultural phenomenon was well underway by the late 1950s and reached completion with the fantastic 1963 Sting Ray. It was thus with great anticipation that the automotive world awaited the 1968 introduction of Chevy's radically revised third-generation model. Enthusiasts were not disappointed with what came to be known as the new C3 Corvette.

Though the new car's chassis was essentially unchanged from previous years, its body and interior were both completely new and cutting edge. Drawing heavily from GM styling chief Bill Mitchell's 1965 Mako Shark II show car, the new look brought Corvette's exaggerated fender peaks and provocative curves to a whole new level, giving the car an aggressive, sexy countenance unlike anything else on the road.

For the first time in Corvette history, coupes featured removable T-tops and a removable back window. T-tops give a convertible-like open-air driving experience with the extra rigidity of a fixed roof, but they are prone to water leakage and are susceptible to rust in the roof's framework. New seals for the T-tops are readily available, but rust in the roof structure is very difficult and expensive to remedy.

As with its exterior, the car's newly styled interior was distinct and exciting. Evocative of a jet fighter, it effectively ensconced both driver and passenger in their own personal cockpit. Excellent reproductions are readily available for all of the soft-trim items, but other interior components, such as the steering wheel, seat frames, and windshield moldings, are not reproduced. As such, it can be difficult and expensive to replace missing or badly damaged items.

With regard to performance, there were few production cars in the world in 1968 that could even approach Corvette. Buyers had their choice of no fewer than seven different engines ranging from the base 327/300 all the way up to the famed L88 option, a race-ready 427 that generated some 580 horsepower. Complementing the engine power were four-wheel disc brakes, four-wheel independent suspension, and a wide variety of performance-oriented options, such as heavy-duty brakes, heavy-duty suspension, off-road exhaust, and transistor ignition.

At the opposite end of the spectrum was a long list of luxury and convenience features. Power steering, brakes, and windows; leather upholstery; telescoping steering column; headrests; air conditioning; speed warning; and AM-FM stereo were but some of the options that permitted buyers to order the grand touring car of their dreams.

As is always the case, well-optioned cars are the most desirable to collectors. Especially valuable are performance-optioned cars, such as those with factory tri-power 427s. At the very top of the value chart are the 80 L88–optioned Corvettes built in 1968.

As was typical of new models, 1968 Corvettes utilize a number of unique, one-year-only parts. These include push button exterior door releases, distinct backup lamps located in the exhaust filler panel, dash-mounted ignition switch, and passenger-side dash panel. Because they were only used one year, 1968-only parts are more expensive and more difficult to find than comparable parts from subsequent years.

Also, as was typical of new models, 1968 Corvettes experienced an inordinate number of problems, which earned them a reputation for poor quality. Squeaks, rattles, and body shimmy were noticeably worse than what was usually found with earlier and later Corvettes. Body panel fit and finish were also worse than usual, with misaligned panels and irregular gaps the norm rather than the exception. Water and wind leaks through the convertible top or T-tops, windshield seal, and side window seals were somewhat common.

Whether these first-year teething pains bear any relation to the quality of a 1968 today is debatable. After so many years have passed, all or most of the problems have usually been addressed more than once. For example, does it matter that body and paint finish were notoriously poor when the car was new if it's been repainted several times since and the example you're looking at has been massaged to perfection? Also, today a well-cared-for or well-restored 1968 will have far less rattles than a poorly cared for or poorly restored 1969.

Today's relevance, then, of 1968's initial shortcomings is not that it is an inferior car in comparison to what followed, but rather that its reputation as an inferior car has somehow survived the decades. And, because people perceive it as such, 1968s don't command as much money as do 1969s, with all else being equal. That, then, makes 1968s something of a comparative bargain, doesn't it?

1968 Corvette Ratings

Model Comfort/Amenities	***
Reliability	****
Collectibility	****
Parts/Service Availability	***
Est. Annual Maintenance Costs	$450

1968 Corvette Replacement Costs for Common Parts

Convertible top w/pads and straps	$210
Windshield (correct reproduction)	$450
Seat upholstery (pair, correct vinyl)	$250
Seat upholstery (pair, correct leather)	$470
Carpet	$275
Door panels (pair, correct reproduction w/out any trim)	$210
Hood (correct press-molded reproduction)	$900
Front fender (correct press-molded reproduction)	$300
Wheel	$125
Headlamp assembly (including cup, ring, adjusters, bezel mount kit, and bulb)	$50
Taillamp housing and lens	$110
Exhaust system	$275
Shock absorber	$75
Front wheel bearing	$15
Front springs (pair)	$100
Brake master cylinder (functional replacement)	$100
Brake caliper (stainless steel sleeved)	$100
Radiator (correct dated reproduction for small-block)	$800
Radiator support	$350
Water pump	$75 (rebuilt original)
Ignition shielding	$360
Cylinder head (pair, small-block rebuildable originals)	$300
Rear leaf spring (functional replacement)	$110
Complete tune-up kit (ignition points, condenser, plugs, distributor cap, rotor, ignition wires)	$60
Fuel tank	$200

1968 Corvette Specifications

Base price (new)	$4,663 (coupe)
	$4,320 (convertible)
Production	9,936 (coupe)
	18,630 (convertible)
Engine	V-8
Bore x stroke (small-block, inches)	4x3.25
Displacement (small-block)	327-ci
Bore x stroke (big-block, inches)	4.25x3.76
Displacement (big-block)	427-ci
Compression ratio	10:1 (base engine)
Horsepower	300 (base engine)
Transmission	3-speed manual standard, 4-speed manual and 3-speed automatic optional
Wheelbase	98 inches
Overall width	69.2 inches
Overall height	47.8 inches
Overall length	182.1 inches
Track, front	58.3 inches
Track, rear	59 inches
Weight	3,440 pounds
Wheels	15x7 inches
Tires	F70x15 bias ply
Front suspension	independent unequal length wishbones and coil springs, anti-sway bar, telescopic shock absorbers
Rear suspension	independent radius arms, transverse leaf spring, half shafts acting as upper locating members, lower transverse rods, telescopic shock absorbers
Steering	recirculating ball
Brakes	4-wheel disc, 4-piston calipers, 11.75-inch rotors front and rear, 461.2 square inches swept area
0 to 60 mph	7.8 seconds (327/300 w/ 3.36:1 axle and 4-speed manual transmission), 6.3 seconds (427/435 w/ 3.55:1 axle and 4-speed manual transmission)
Standing 1/4-mile	16 seconds @ 86.5 mph (327/300 w/ 3.36:1 axle and 4-speed manual transmission), 14.1 seconds @ 103 mph (427/435 w/ 3.55:1 axle and 4-speed manual transmission)
Top speed	121 mph (327/300 w/ 3.36:1 axle and 4-speed manual transmission), 160 mph (427/435 w/ 3.55:1 axle and 4-speed manual transmission)

The 1968 model year was the first for removable T-tops and a removable back window. These features were offered on coupes only.

1968 Corvette Major Options

		Quantity	Price
A01	Tinted glass	17,635	$15.80
A02	Tinted windshield	5,509	$10.55
A31	Power windows	7,065	$57.95
A82	Head restraints	3,197	$42.15
A85	Custom shoulder harness	350	$26.35
C07	Auxiliary hardtop	8,735	$231.75
C08	Auxiliary hardtop vinyl covering	3,050	$52.70
C50	Rear window defroster	693	$31.60
C60	Air conditioning	5,664	$412.90
F41	Special performance suspension	1,758	$36.90
G81	Positraction rear axle	27,008	$46.35
J50	Vacuum power brakes	9,559	$42.15
J56	Heavy-duty brakes	81	$384.45
K66	Transistor ignition	5,457	$73.75
L30	327/300-horsepower engine	5,875	base engine
L36	427/390-horsepower engine	7,717	$200.15
L68	427/400-horsepower engine	1,932	$305.50
L71	427/435-horsepower engine	2,898	$437.10
L79	327/350-horsepower engine	9,440	$105.35
L88	427/430-horsepower engine	80	$947.90
L89	427/435-horsepower engine w/aluminum cylinder heads	624	$805.75
M20	4-speed wide-ratio manual transmission	10,760	$184.35
M21	4-speed close-ratio manual transmission	12,337	$184.35
M22	4-speed heavy-duty manual transmission	80	$263.30
M40	Turbo Hydra-Matic transmission	5,063	$226.45
N11	Off-road exhaust	4,695	$36.90
N36	Telescopic steering column	6,477	$42.15
N40	Power steering	12,364	$94.80
PT6	F70-15 red stripe tires	11,686	$31.30
PT7	F70-15 white stripe tires	9,692	$31.30
P01	Wheel trim covers	8,971	$57.95
UA6	Horn alarm system	388	$26.35
U15	Speed warning indicator	3,453	$10.55
U69	AM-FM radio	27,920	$172.75
U79	Stereo equipment	3,311	$278.10
	Leather interior trim	2,429	$79.00

In the good ol' days, it was highly fashionable to remove emissions control apparatus and throw it away. Today, collectors want cars to appear exactly as they did when they left the factory, smog equipment included. Air injection reaction pump systems and other emissions equipment are difficult to find and expensive to buy, something to consider when examining a car.

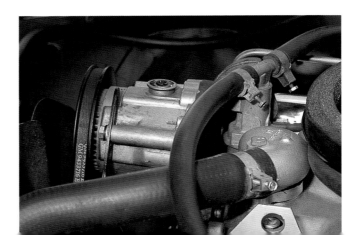

A total of only 80 Corvettes came with option L88 in 1968. This was essentially a road-racing option package that included an aluminum head 427 engine, which produced somewhere in the neighborhood of 580 horsepower. As you would expect, surviving L88s command a fantastic premium in the marketplace, with quality examples easily fetching well over $100,000.

All else equal, convertibles are more desirable than coupes in today's marketplace and as such will typically sell for upwards of 50 percent more.

In addition to the base unit, there were six optional engines offered in 1968. Factory big blocks, especially tri-power 427/435-horsepower examples, are extremely popular with collectors.

Whether a vintage Corvette has its original engine block can dramatically influence its value. The engine stamping, located on a pad just rearward of the water pump on the passenger side, is key to determining originality of the block. Be aware that altering the stamping, or restamping, is a fairly common practice.

The presence or absence of correct components can significantly affect the value of a vintage Corvette. If you are seeking a correct car, thoroughly familiarize yourself with details such as the original upholstery pattern, carpet pad configuration, and component finishes.

Long gone are the days when a steam clean and spray-can paint job constituted an engine compartment "restoration." Though time consuming and expensive to accomplish, correct, high-quality detailing is demanded by today's discerning collectors. If this level of restoration is important to you, expect to pay a premium for it when buying a car.

In general, non-stock items tend to detract from the value of vintage Corvettes. Easily replaced bolt-on parts like these period-correct wheels typically don't impair value and, in fact, may even enhance it to some people.

What They Said in 1968

Beautifully styled, lusty, exciting—Chevy's Corvette coupe is the automobile world's Barbarella. —*Car and Driver,* May 1968

Long, low, wide, sleek, this 1968 sport coupe is endowed with smooth ferocity. —*Car Life,* November 1967

I Bought a 1968 Corvette

I remember when the 1968s came out and how much excitement they generated. I was still in high school, so of course I could only dream about owning a Corvette later in life. In 1990, I set out looking for a 1968 in particular, because that's the year that really ignited my love affair with Corvette. I bought my convertible from a reputable dealer, and it's been a totally positive experience so far. It drives and rides as good as any thirty-plus-year-old car. I've had to restore the brake system and install a new convertible top, but those are the only major things I've done. I drive the car a lot in the warm weather and very little in the winter, and have clocked over 27,000 miles. —Edward Chang

1968 Garage Watch

Evaluating the function of mechanical parts begins with a careful visual inspection. Fluid around the steering box, brake-line fittings, master cylinder, radiator, expansion tank, fuel pump, or just about anywhere else is indicative of trouble.

The bumps in the body between the hood and headlamps indicate a serious corrosion problem with this car. When the rivets holding the fiberglass bonding strips to the metal support beneath this part of the body corrode, their heads swell and cause the bumps to appear.

The 1968 models have more one-year-only components than any other C3s. This makes them more expensive and somewhat more difficult to restore. Examples of unique components include backup lamps, door handles, dash pads, seats, and parking brake console surround.

Rust in the fuel tank is a common problem in all C3 Corvettes, including 1968s. Check for rust on the inside of the tank by looking through the filler opening.

Vacuum motors raised and lowered headlamps. The extensive network of vacuum lines and related hardware needed for this system is prone to leaks and can be time consuming to diagnose.

A series of relatively small problems can add up to a large restoration bill, something to consider when evaluating a prospective purchase. Replacing droopy exterior door handles, a very common problem, will set you back about $110 per side.

The year 1969 was a banner one for Corvette, with a record setting 38,762 cars built. A wide variety of options, including luxuries like air conditioning and ultra-performance big-block engines, such as the L71 and L88, allowed buyers to order a car that suited their specific preferences. The great variety of offerings, classic Stingray styling, outstanding performance, and ease of use that 1969s offer make them favorites with collectors.

The second year for Chevy's C3 Corvette benefited from a number of refinements. The separate finger grab and push button door opener introduced in 1968 were combined into one mechanism, front fenders got a "Stingray" emblem, and separate backup lamps were eliminated in favor of new ones integrated into the inboard taillamps.

As was true for all 1968 through 1972 Corvettes, cars with any of the optional 427 engines were fitted with a unique hood. It had a larger central bulge than the small-block hood, two sections of bright trim, and "427" emblems on both sides of the bulge. Bright, silver trim for the front fender vents and chrome-covered side exhaust were both 1969-only options. Though tire size remained the same as before, wheel width increased from 7 to 8 inches.

Interior layout was basically the same as 1968, though a number of improvements were added. Previously optional headrests became standard, the ignition switch moved to the steering column, steering wheel diameter was reduced from 16 to 15 inches, and map pockets were added to the passenger-side dash.

Corvette's 1969 engine lineup was arguably the best in the marque's history. The base powerplant displaced 350-ci and produced 300 horsepower. At extra cost, buyers could have a 350/350 or any one of six different 427 engines. The selection began with relatively mild big-block engines rated at 390 horsepower for one with a single four-barrel and hydraulic lifters, and 400 horsepower for the same engine with three two-barrel Holley carburetors atop an aluminum intake manifold. Next came two high-compression, hot-cammed renditions. Both featured tri-power and were rated at 435 horsepower, but the more desirable L89-optioned version sported aluminum cylinder heads in place of the L71's iron heads. At the top of the ladder were the famed L88 and ZL1 engines. Both were essentially all-out road-racing option packages that were identical, except the ZL1 got an aluminum engine block instead of the L88's iron block. Unlike in 1967 and 1968, these racing engines could be ordered with an automatic transmission, but they still could

not be had with air conditioning, a radio, or a heater.

This was the last year that Corvettes came standard with a three-speed manual transmission, and only 252 cars were so equipped. As in 1968, GM's three-speed Turbo Hydra-Matic automatic was optional. A stronger version of the automatic was utilized when it was coupled with one of the high-horsepower big-block engines.

The 1969 Corvettes are perennial favorites with collectors. As is always the case, high-optioned and high-performance examples command the most attention. When properly documented as factory original, unusual option combinations such as 427/400 engine, air conditioning, and four-speed in a convertible fetch princely sums.

Like all C3 Corvettes, 1969s had a build sheet glued on top of the gas tank at the factory. Commonly called a tank sticker, it is highly prized by collectors and is particularly important for rare and desirable cars. Other valuable documentation can include the car's original window sticker, warranty booklet, order form, shipper, and invoice. Be aware, however, that all of these documents are being reproduced. It takes an expert's eye to discern the difference between originals and reproductions.

Despite their age, 1969s are still easy cars to drive on an everyday basis. Options such as power steering, power brakes, and power windows, plus air conditioning and AM/FM stereo, make them a pleasure to drive.

Common ailments to watch out for when buying a 1969 include rust in the chassis, windshield frame, and radiator support. Leaky brake calipers, malfunctioning headlamps or windshield wiper door mechanisms, and sagging rear springs are also fairly common.

As is always a good idea when buying a several-decades-old car, don't forget to check the function of everything when considering a purchase. Make sure all instruments, the radio, HVAC controls, lights, and horns all function as they should. Take a close look at all of the weatherstrips, including the seals around the convertible top or T-tops. Make certain that the spare tire, which is supposed to be located in a fiberglass tub mounted between the mufflers, is present. Do the same for the jack and lug wrench, both of which should be in the storage compartment behind the passenger seat.

Virtually any part you might need to replace is available, but it may cost you. Take this into careful consideration when evaluating a prospective purchase.

1969 Corvette Ratings

Model Comfort/Amenities	***
Reliability	****
Collectibility	*****
Parts/Service Availability	****
Est. Annual Maintenance Costs	$450

1969 Corvette Replacement Costs for Common Parts

Convertible top w/ pads and straps	$210
Windshield (correct reproduction)	$450
Seat upholstery (pair, correct vinyl)	$250
Seat upholstery (pair, correct leather)	$460
Carpet	$275
Door panels (pair, correct reproduction w/out trim)	$230
Hood (correct press-molded reproduction)	$900
Front fender (correct press-molded reproduction)	$300
Wheel	$125
Headlamp assembly (including cup, ring, adjusters, bezel mount kit, and bulb)	$50
Taillamp housing and lens	$110
Exhaust system	$275
Shock absorber	$75
Front wheel bearing	$15
Front springs (pair)	$100
Brake master cylinder (functional replacement)	$100
Brake caliper (stainless steel sleeved)	$100
Radiator (correct dated reproduction for small-block)	$800
Radiator support	$350
Water pump	$75 (rebuilt original)
Ignition shielding	$360
Cylinder head (pair, small-block rebuildable originals)	$300
Rear leaf spring (functional replacement)	$110
Complete tune-up kit (ignition points, condenser, plugs, distributor cap, rotor, ignition wires)	$60
Fuel tank	$200

1969 Corvette Specifications

Base price (new)	$4,763 (coupe)
	$4,420 (convertible)
Production	22,129 (coupe)
	16,633 (convertible)
Engine	V-8
Bore x stroke (small-block, inches)	4x3.48
Displacement (small-block)	350-ci
Bore x stroke (big-block, inches)	4.25x3.76
Displacement (big-block)	427-ci
Compression ratio	10.25:1 (base engine)
Horsepower	300 (base engine)
Transmission	3-speed manual standard, 4-speed manual, and 3-speed automatic optional
Wheelbase	98 inches
Overall width	69.2 inches
Overall height	47.8 inches
Overall length	182.1 inches
Track, front	58.7 inches
Track, rear	59.4 inches
Weight	3,450 pounds
Wheels	15x8 inches
Tires	F70x15 bias ply
Front suspension	independent unequal length wishbones and coil springs, anti-sway bar, telescopic shock absorbers
Rear suspension	independent radius arms, transverse leaf spring, half shafts acting as upper locating members, lower transverse rods, telescopic shock absorbers
Steering	recirculating ball
Brakes	4-wheel disc, 4-piston calipers, 11.75-inch rotors front and rear, 461.2 square inches swept area
0 to 60 mph	7.8 seconds (350/300 w/ 3.36:1 axle and 4-speed manual transmission), 5.3 seconds (427/435 w/ 3.70:1 axle and 4-speed manual transmission)
Standing 1/4-mile	14.6 seconds @ 98.4 mph (350/300 w/ 3.36:1 axle and 4-speed manual transmission), 13.8 seconds @ 106.8 mph (427/435 w/ 3.70:1 axle and 4-speed manual transmission)
Top speed	126 mph (350/300 w/ 3.36:1 axle and 4-speed manual transmission), 138 mph (427/435 w/ 3.70:1 axle and 4-speed manual transmission)

The stock big-block hood featured "427" emblems and a bigger power bulge than the small-block hood, but chrome-trimmed vents were not functional.

1969 Corvette Major Options

		Quantity	Price
A01	Tinted glass	31,270	$16.90
A31	Power windows	9,816	$63.20
A82	Head restraints	38,762	$17.95
A85	Custom shoulder harness	600	$42.15
C07	Auxiliary hardtop	7,878	$252.80
C08	Auxiliary hardtop vinyl trim	3,266	$57.95
C50	Rear window defroster	2,485	$32.65
C60	Air conditioning	11,859	$428.70
F41	Special performance suspension	1,661	$36.90
G81	Positraction rear axle	36,965	$46.35
J50	Vacuum power brakes	16,876	$42.15
J56	Heavy-duty brakes	115	$384.45
K05	Engine-block heater	824	$10.55
K66	Transistor ignition	5,702	$81.10
L36	427/390-horsepower engine	10,531	$221.20
L46	350/350-horsepower engine	12,846	$131.65
L68	427/400-horsepower engine	2,072	$326.55
L71	427/435-horsepower engine	2,722	$437.10
L88	427/430-horsepower engine	116	$1,032.15
L89	427/435-horsepower engine w/ aluminum cylinder heads	390	$832.05
MA6	Heavy-duty clutch	102	$79
M20	4-speed wide-ratio manual transmission	16,507	$184.80
M21	4-speed close-ratio manual transmission	13,741	$184.80
M22	4-speed heavy-duty manual transmission	101	$290.40
M40	Turbo Hydra-Matic transmission	8,161	$221.80
	(M40 Turbo Hydra-Matic automatic w/ L71, L88, or L89 engine option		$290.40)
N14	Side-mounted exhaust	4,355	$147.45
N37	Tilt & Telescopic steering column	10,325	$84.30
N40	Power steering	22,866	$105.35
PT6	F70-15 red stripe tires	5,210	$31.30
PT7	F70-15 white stripe tires	21,379	$31.30
PU9	F70-15 white lettered tires	2,398	$33.15
PO2	Deluxe wheel trim covers	8,073	$57.95
UA6	Horn alarm system	12,436	$26.35
U15	Speed warning indicator	3,561	$11.60
U69	AM/FM radio	37,985	$172.75
U79	Stereo equipment	4,114	$278.10
ZL1	Special aluminum 427 engine	2	$3,000
	Leather interior trim	3,729	$79

This factory-installed side-pipe system was available only in 1969, but it will function on other C3 Corvettes. It is a very desirable feature on 1969s if the car originally came with it. The outer chrome cover is separated from the actual pipe by a fiberglass insulator to prevent it from getting too hot.

The tri-power engine was offered in two different states of tune. The high-compression, hot-cam version delivered a pavement-scorching 435 horsepower, while the milder version produced "only" 400 horsepower. Until many years later when the ZR1 came along, the latter was the highest-horsepower engine that could be ordered along with air conditioning. The "400-horse air cars," as collectors call them, are highly prized.

Optional deluxe wheel covers and front fender louver trim really dresses up the exterior. The fancy wheel covers were optional through 1973, but the fender trim was a 1969-only offering.

The interior of the 1969s continued the jet fighter theme introduced the previous year. Virtually everything needed to restore this interior is readily available, but a complete rehab, not including labor, will set you back a couple of thousand dollars.

Though taboo for serious show cars, modern radial tires do wonders to improve the handling and ride quality of vintage Corvettes.

The 1969 Corvettes are very popular with the vintage-racing crowd. Some of these cars can readily do double duty as weekend warriors and street cars, while others are suitable only for track use.

When considering an ultra-rare collectible such as one of the 116 L88s built in 1969, you are best off enlisting the assistance of an expert if you do not have considerable expertise yourself. Fraud is an issue in the entire collector-car hobby, and when it comes to high-dollar cars such as an L88, it is even more of a problem.

What They Said in 1969

Its excellent engineering tends to be obscured by some rather garish styling gimmick. The small-engined Corvettes are marginally fast and extraordinarily civilized. The large-engined Corvettes are extraordinarily fast and marginally civilized. —*Car and Driver,* October 1968

I Bought a 1969 Corvette

Over the years, I've owned six different 1969 Corvettes and presently have two, a 350/350 small-block coupe and a 427/435 big-block convertible. If you like the Stingray body style, 1969 is the one to have, in my opinion. It combines the best option choices, the cleanest styling, and the best color choices. There is nothing like the grunt of a big-block, and it gets the most attention at car shows, but honestly, the small-block is a much better driver. It has air conditioning, which wasn't available with the 435-horsepower engine, never runs hot, and handles considerably better. —Ross Hayes

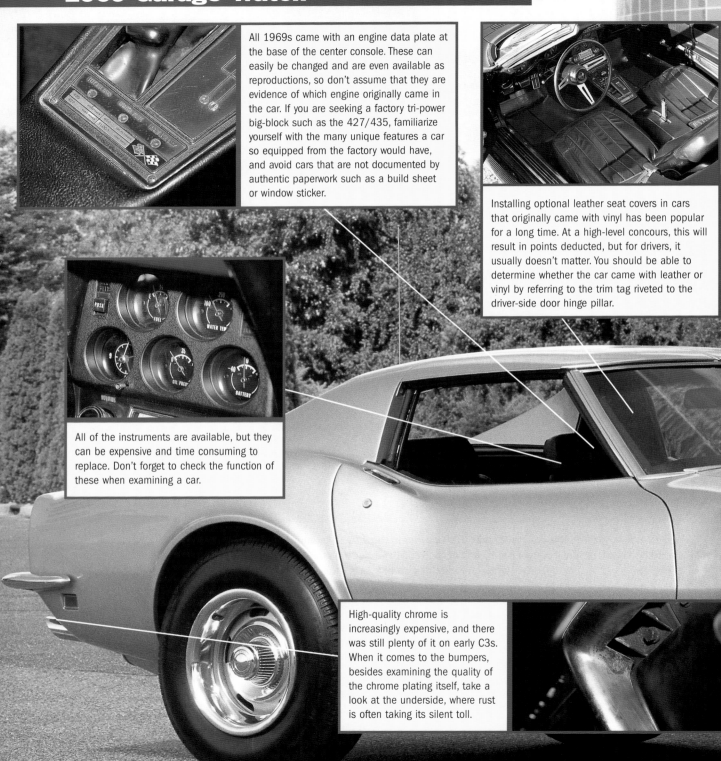

All 1969s came with an engine data plate at the base of the center console. These can easily be changed and are even available as reproductions, so don't assume that they are evidence of which engine originally came in the car. If you are seeking a factory tri-power big-block such as the 427/435, familiarize yourself with the many unique features a car so equipped from the factory would have, and avoid cars that are not documented by authentic paperwork such as a build sheet or window sticker.

Installing optional leather seat covers in cars that originally came with vinyl has been popular for a long time. At a high-level concours, this will result in points deducted, but for drivers, it usually doesn't matter. You should be able to determine whether the car came with leather or vinyl by referring to the trim tag riveted to the driver-side door hinge pillar.

All of the instruments are available, but they can be expensive and time consuming to replace. Don't forget to check the function of these when examining a car.

High-quality chrome is increasingly expensive, and there was still plenty of it on early C3s. When it comes to the bumpers, besides examining the quality of the chrome plating itself, take a look at the underside, where rust is often taking its silent toll.

The base Corvette came without a radio, but for an additional cost, an AM-FM radio or AM-FM stereo could be ordered. Ordinarily, the absence of a desirable feature such as a radio is a detriment, but one notable exception is when a car has been ordered with the highest-performance engine of them all, the L88 option. In that case, buyers were not permitted to get a radio even if they wanted one.

Even the high-performance big-block engines came with AIR pumps in 1969, and the absence of this or any other emissions regulating components should be noted when you are considering a car for purchase. If the car is an ordinary driver or a custom, this will probably not be a big issue. However, if it is a stock, high-end showpiece, you may wind up spending a couple of thousand dollars to replace missing smog equipment.

Installing non-stock hoods has been popular with Corvettes since the beginning. Though the hood is a bolt-on item, originals are expensive and, of course, need to be painted to match the car, which sometimes presents a problem. Keep this in mind if the car you are considering had its hood changed.

Corvette production was extended for the 1969 model year, and 1970 production did not begin until January 1970. Because of the shortened model year, only 17,316 Corvettes were built in 1970, the lowest production number since 1962.

The Corvette was further refined both inside and out for 1970. The exterior is easily distinguished from previous years by the integral flares in the body panels behind each wheel. These eliminated the paint damage that resulted from the tires throwing road debris rearward. Redesigned fender vents and front body grilles, both of which featured an egg-crate pattern, also differentiate 1970s from earlier Stingrays.

Minor revisions to the interior included new seat designs and a new custom interior trim option package. This option included leather seat covers, plusher carpet, wood grain accents and carpet trim on the bottoms of the door panels, and wood grain accents on the center console.

Corvette's base engine remained a 350/300, and a new 370 horsepower small-block option called LT1 was introduced. It was built from heavy-duty components, and with its 11:1 compression, big Holley four-barrel, large-valve heads, and aggressive camshaft profile, it revved willingly all the way up to its 6,500-rpm redline. Its desirable combination of high power and relatively light weight made it one of the fastest, best-handling Corvettes of the era. Because of this, it was an instant classic and remains a favorite with collectors today.

A longer-stroke crankshaft for Corvette's big-block resulted in a displacement increase to 454-ci. A potent new version called option LS7 was scheduled to debut in 1970, but it was cancelled before any were built. Helped along by high-compression pistons, a big Holley four-barrel, racy cam, and aluminum heads, it was to be rated at 460 horsepower.

The lone big-block that did make it to production for 1970 was a single four-barrel with 10.25:1 compression and hydraulic lifters. Though this engine, called LS5, still made enough power and torque to make Corvettes so equipped the quickest production cars of the time, the golden era of musclecars was clearly coming to a close.

The most desirable 1970s are convertibles with LT1 or LS5 and lots of other options. As is always the case with especially rare and valuable cars, authentic documentation evidencing the originality of options is increasingly important to collectors. Because most forms of documentation are being reproduced, determine the authenticity of any paperwork that accompanies a car. This is a task that should be entrusted to someone intimately familiar with the characteristics of original paperwork.

Originality of the car's engine block and other components is also very important to most collectors. Many major components, including the engine, came from the factory with the car's serial number and various other important data stamped or cast in. Restamping of engines is a common occurrence, and, as with evaluating the authenticity of documentation, determining the authenticity of an engine stamping is best left to an expert if the stamping is in fact important to you.

When considering a car for purchase, take a close look at those areas prone to rust. These include the chassis side rails, windshield frame, and radiator support. Also carefully examine the body for evidence of collision damage and poor-quality repairs. The best way to do this is by scrutinizing the body panels from underneath. Factory panels should be a very dark gray and should be unpainted and uncoated almost everywhere. If the panels are a different color, then it is certain that they were changed. If the undersides of the panels are painted or are blanketed with undercoating, you should be suspicious that someone has tried to hide something.

Also examine the underside of the body along the seams where adjacent panels are joined. The factory bonding strips that overlap adjacent panels should be dark-gray fiberglass, and the bonding adhesive should also be a very dark gray or dull black. Breaks in the bonding strips or a different color adhesive are sure signs of repair. A complete absence of bonding strips and seams indicates the presence of a one-piece, molded body section. This was a fairly common repair technique that is highly frowned upon by enthusiasts today.

Besides looking at the cosmetics, be sure to evaluate the function of all components and systems. Though some parts are quite expensive to replace, in many instances the cost of the labor needed to accomplish the installation is far greater than the price of the part. A good example of this is a simple vacuum leak that can be fixed with a few dollars worth of new hose. Given the pervasiveness and complexity of Corvette's vacuum systems, which include emissions controls, HVAC controls, headlamp housing, and windshield wiper door controls, the time to locate and access a leaking hose can be lengthy.

1970 Corvette Ratings

Model Comfort/Amenities	***
Reliability ****	
Collectibility	*****
Parts/Service Availability	****
Est. Annual Maintenance Costs	$450

1970 Corvette Replacement Costs for Common Parts

Convertible top w/ pads and straps	$210
Windshield (correct reproduction)	$450
Seat upholstery (pair, correct vinyl)	$250
Seat upholstery (pair, correct leather)	$460
Carpet	$275
Door panels (pair, correct reproduction w/out any trim)	$210
Hood (correct press-molded reproduction)	$900
Front fender (correct press-molded reproduction)	$300
Wheel	$125
Headlamp assembly (including cup, ring, adjusters, bezel mount kit, and bulb)	$50
Taillamp housing and lens	$110
Exhaust system	$275
Shock absorber	$75
Front wheel bearing	$15
Front springs (pair)	$100
Brake master cylinder (functional replacement)	$100
Brake caliper (stainless steel sleeved)	$100
Radiator (correct dated reproduction for small-block)	$800
Radiator support	$350
Water pump	$75 (rebuilt original)
Ignition shielding	$360
Cylinder head (pair)	$300 (small-block rebuildable originals)
Rear leaf spring (functional replacement)	$110
Complete tune-up kit (ignition points, condenser, plugs, distributor cap, rotor, ignition wires)	$60
Fuel tank	$200

1970 Corvette Specifications

Base price (new)	$5,192 (coupe)
	$4,849 (convertible)
Production	10,668 (coupe)
	6,648 (convertible)
Engine	V-8
Bore x stroke (small-block, inches)	4x3.48
Displacement (small-block)	350-ci
Bore x stroke (big-block, inches	4.25x4
Displacement (big-block)	454-ci
Compression ratio	10.25:1 (base engine)
Horsepower	300 (base engine)
Transmission	4-speed wide-ratio manual standard, 4-speed close-ratio manual and 3-speed automatic optional
Wheelbase	98 inches
Overall width	69 inches
Overall height	47.5 inches
Overall length	182.5 inches
Track, front	58.7 inches
Track, rear	59.4 inches
Weight	3,400 pounds
Wheels	15x8 inches
Tires	F70x15 bias ply
Front suspension	independent unequal length wishbones and coil springs, anti-sway bar, telescopic shock absorbers
Rear suspension	independent radius arms, transverse leaf spring, half shafts acting as upper locating members, lower transverse rods, telescopic shock absorbers
Steering	recirculating ball
Brakes	4-wheel disc, 4-piston calipers, 11.75-inch rotors front and rear, 461.2 square inches swept area.
0 to 60 mph	7.6 seconds (350/300 w/ 3.36:1 axle and 4-speed manual transmission), 5.7 seconds (350/370 w/ 4.11:1 axle and 4-speed manual transmission)
Standing 1/4-mile	14.5 seconds @ 98.8 mph (350/370 w/ 3.36:1 axle and 4-speed manual transmission), 14.17 seconds @ 102.15 mph (350/370 w/ 4.11:1 axle and 4-speed manual transmission)
Top speed	125 mph (350/300 w/ 3.36:1 axle and 4-speed manual transmission), 122 mph (350/370 w/ 4.11:1 axle and 4-speed manual transmission)

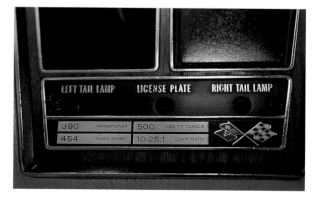

Engine compression began to diminish in 1970. The LS5, the highest-performance engine in the Corvette lineup that year, relied on 10.25:1 compression. This was still high enough to make a lot of power but low enough to operate satisfactorily on today's premium pump fuel.

Optional deluxe wheel covers, installed on 3,467 Corvettes in 1970, are surprisingly heavy and complex. Also used on other GM vehicles of the era, they dramatically change the car's appearance.

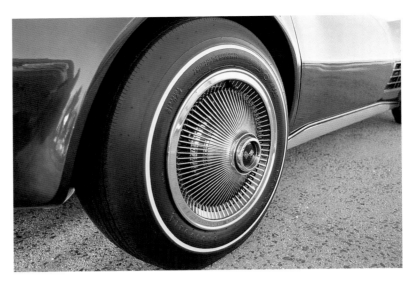

Molded-in fender flares, egg-crate-style fender vents and front grilles, and chrome bumpers front and rear characterize 1970 through 1972 styling.

1970 Corvette Major Options

		Quantity	Price
A31	Power windows	4,813	$63.20
A85	Custom shoulder harness	475	$42.15
C07	Auxiliary hardtop	2,556	$273.85
C08	Auxiliary hardtop vinyl trim	832	$63.20
C50	Rear window defroster	1,281	$36.90
C60	Air conditioning	6,659	$447.65
G81	Optional positraction axle ratio	2,862	$12.65
J50	Vacuum power brakes	8,984	$47.40
L46	350/350-horsepower engine	4,910	$158
LS5	454/390-horsepower engine	4,473	$289.65
LT1	350/370-horsepower engine	1,287	$447.60
M21	4-speed close-ratio manual transmission	4,383	no charge
M22	4-speed heavy-duty manual transmission	25	$95
M40	Turbo Hydra-Matic transmission	5,102	no charge
NA9	California emissions equipment		$36.90
N37	Tilt & Telescopic steering column	5,803	$84.30
N40	Power steering	11,907	$105.35
PT7	F70-15 white stripe nylon tires	6,589	$31.30
PU9	F70-15 White letter nylon tires	7,985	$33.15
P02	Deluxe wheel trim covers	3,467	$57.95
T60	Heavy-duty battery	165	$15.80
UA6	Horn alarm system	6,727	$31.60
U69	AM-FM radio	16,991	$172.75
U79	Stereo equipment	2,462	$278.10
ZR1	Special-purpose 350 engine package*	25	$968.95
	Custom interior trim	3,191	$158

*Option ZR1 is a road-racing package that includes an LT1 engine, stiffer front and rear springs, heavy-duty shock absorbers, a special Harrison aluminum radiator (part number 3007436), an M22 4-speed transmission, and a heavy-duty brake package. The brake package includes twin-pin front calipers, an extra support for each front caliper, a proportioning valve, and metallic brake pads. N40 power steering, A31 power windows, P02 wheel covers, C50 rear window defroster, and C60 air conditioning could not be ordered with the ZR1 package.

All 1970 Corvette coupes were equipped with lap and shoulder belts, while convertibles came with lapbelts as standard and shoulder belts as an extra-cost option.

Though the 1970's chassis design dates back to the original 1963 Sting Ray, continuous refinements make it noticeably better. Suitably optioned C3s are fun to drive and are user-friendly enough to serve as everyday transportation.

Standard seat upholstery was a combination of slightly grained flat vinyl with Chevrolet's comfort-weave vinyl inserts sewn into the seat bottoms and backs. Leather was available as an extra-cost option but only in black or saddle.

Virtually everything you may need to restore your 1970 interior is readily available, but the cost adds up quickly. As with everything else, you are usually better off paying more for a car that has a good interior rather than one in need of serious work.

This is the unrestored engine compartment of a 35,000-mile car. This level of originality is highly prized by collectors, and you should expect to pay a premium for an original car in excellent condition.

What They Said in 1970

There is Corvette and there is Porsche. One is the best engineering effort of America, the other of Germany. The difference in machines is not as great as the disparity in price. —*Motor Trend,* May 1970

I Bought a 1970 Corvette

I've owned my 1970 convertible for eight years, and it has been something of a love-hate relationship. The car was previously owned by a dentist who didn't have time for it, so he let it sit outside for about ten years without touching it. Needless to say, it needed just about everything, from paint, to brakes, to an engine rebuild. Naturally, getting the car back into pristine condition has taken a lot more effort, time, and money than I expected. Now that it's basically done I can say it was worth it, but I seriously doubt I'd go through that level of restoration again. —Jack McCrean

1970 Garage Watch

Many buyers tend to overlook details when evaluating a car. Spend the extra time needed to thoroughly examine all the details, especially if you are buying a higher-end car that will be seriously shown. Correct headlamp bulbs will set you back about $200. Adding the cost to remedy 10 or 20 relatively small items can yield a bill of several thousand dollars.

Corvette's engine compartment became increasingly crowded and complicated as time went on. You are always better off buying a car with its many underhood hoses, wires, and components intact.

All 1970 Corvettes came with inertia reel-type retracting seat belts. Make sure the belts are present, the retractor mechanism works smoothly, and the belts lock when they are pulled suddenly.

This is the deluxe door panel, distinguished by simulated wood trim and the carpeted area along the bottom. Door panels are prone to cracking in the armrest area. Minor cracks can be repaired with satisfactory results, but more significant damage necessitates replacement.

The mileage on a vintage Corvette is only relevant insofar as you can document that it is accurate. The odometer may have stopped working (usually due to failure of its plastic gears), or an unscrupulous owner may have simply disconnected the speedometer cable, resulting in a reading that does not reflect actual miles traveled. That is why condition and authenticity is usually more important than indicated mileage.

Original paperwork, such as the window sticker, build sheet, and warranty booklet, is highly desirable to collectors and enhances the value of a vintage Corvette.

The brake calipers utilized on 1965 through 1982 Corvettes are susceptible to corrosion in their piston bores. Fluid present on the chassis side of the wheels and tires is a sure sign of leaking brakes. The proper fix entails installation of stainless steel sleeved calipers.

Despite de-tuned engines designed to run on lower-octane, unleaded fuel, performance of 1971 Corvettes changed little from the previous year.

From a styling perspective, 1971s were little changed from the previous year. They continued to feature a "square motif" to various body parts, including the exhaust tips and exhaust tip openings, front parking lights, front and rear side marker lamps, egg-crate pattern front grills, and corresponding egg-crate shaped front fender vents.

One element that did distinguish the 1971 model year's exterior from its predecessors was increased quality in both fit and finish. Body improvements began with a reformulated resin mixture used to create the fiberglass body panels. According to Chevrolet, this new mixture, dubbed low-profile resin by plant personnel, was "nearly as smooth as any steel component could be."

As with its exterior, the 1971 interior was nearly unchanged from the previous year. The fiber optic light-monitoring system, which let the driver know if any exterior lamps were not functioning, made its final appearance in 1971. It is thought that the fiber optics were eliminated to offset the cost of the anti-theft alarm system, which became standard equipment in 1972.

Shoulder belts, which were standard on coupes but optional on convertibles, passed through a slot in the seatbacks and anchored in inertia reels located out of sight in the rear of the body. This made for a neat appearance by creating the impression that the shoulder belts were built right into the seats.

In keeping with the Corvette's evolution from a somewhat austere, pure sporting machine to a luxury GT car, custom interior trim continued as an option in 1971. This dress-up package, available only in black or saddle, featured deep pile carpeting, leather-trimmed seats, special door panels with a strip of carpeting along the bottom, and wood grain trim behind the door pull, matching wood grain trim on the center console, and a leather shift boot when the standard transmission was specified.

Underhood offerings for 1971 were pretty exciting, no small accomplishment considering the mandates coursing into Detroit from Washington, D.C. The disappearance of leaded fuel was imminent, and without lead to lubricate upper-engine components and boost octane ratings, compression ratios would drop accordingly. Early in 1970, GM president Edward Cole announced that all 1971 GM cars, including Corvettes, would have to run on fuel with a research octane number no higher than 91. This meant, in practical terms, that engine compression ratios would be no higher than 9:1.

The base 350 engine generated a still-respectable 270 horsepower, while Chevy's venerable LT1 small-block, hampered by a compression drop to 9:1, produced 330 horsepower, a loss of 40 horsepower from the 1970 model's 370-horsepower rating. But even at that, the solid-lifter, performance-cammed LT1 could still willingly rev all the way up to its 6,500-rpm redline.

On the big-block front, Chevrolet offered two 454 engines in 1971. The LS5 featured 8.5:1 compression and hydraulic lifters, and generated 365 horsepower and a ground-scorching 465 lbs-ft of torque at a very tractable 3,200 rpm.

The second big-block on the option sheet for 1971 was something of an anomaly. Dubbed LS6, this spiritual successor to the L88/ZL1/LS7 engines sported aluminum heads and heavy-duty internals. Despite a modest 9.0:1 compression ratio, it still produced 425 horsepower.

Though many decried Corvette's diminishing performance in 1971 and subsequent years, the reality is that 1971s are virtually as fast as 1970s in real-world driving situations. Furthermore, unlike with earlier high-compression, high-performance powerplants, 1971's lower-compression engines are more agreeable to today's pump gas.

While increased drivability and comfort add to the desirability of 1971s, they still suffer from certain problems to look out for. Rust in the chassis and its components, including trailing arms, radiator support, and windshield frame, is perhaps the most common serious ailment.

Also beware of corrosion in the body's front-header support. This is a steel box section bonded to the underside of the nose section's fiberglass between the headlights and hood. The box section itself can hold water and rust from the inside out. In addition, the aluminum rivets that hold the fiberglass bonding strips that go between the support and fiberglass nose sometimes corrode. This causes them to swell, resulting in bumps in the fiberglass.

Breaks in the cables that comprise the fiber optic system and vacuum leaks in Corvette's pervasive vacuum system are other problems seen with some regularity. As always, besides keeping an eye out for Corvette-specific maladies, don't forget to check the function of all systems and components in any car you are considering for purchase.

1971 Corvette Ratings

Model Comfort/Amenities	***
Reliability ****	
Collectibility	*****
Parts/Service Availability	****
Est. Annual Repair Costs	$450

1971 Corvette Replacement Costs for Common Parts

Convertible top w/ pads and straps	$210
Windshield (correct reproduction)	$450
Seat upholstery (pair, correct vinyl)	$250
Seat upholstery (pair, correct leather)	$460
Carpet	$275
Door panels (pair, correct reproduction w/out trim)	$210
Hood (correct press-molded reproduction)	$900
Front fender (correct press-molded reproduction)	$300
Wheel	$125
Headlamp assembly (including cup, ring, adjusters, bezel mount kit, and bulb)	$50
Taillamp housing and lens	$110
Exhaust system	$275
Shock absorber	$75
Front wheel bearing	$15
Front springs (pair)	$100
Brake master cylinder (functional replacement)	$100
Brake caliper (stainless steel sleeved)	$100
Radiator (correct dated reproduction for small-block)	$800
Radiator support	$350
Water pump	$75 (rebuilt original)
Ignition shielding	$360
Cylinder head (pair, small-block rebuildable originals)	$300
Rear leaf spring (functional replacement)	$110
Complete tune-up kit (ignition points, condenser, plugs, distributor cap, rotor, ignition wires)	$60
Fuel tank	$200

1971 Corvette Specifications

Base price (new)	$5,496 (coupe)
	$5,259 (convertible)
Production	14,680 (coupe)
	7,120 (convertible)
Engine	V-8
Bore x stroke (small-block, inches)	4x3.48
Displacement (small-block)	350-ci
Bore x stroke (big-block, inches)	4.25x4
Displacement (big-block)	454-ci
Compression ratio	8.5:1 (base engine)
Horsepower	270 (base engine)
Transmission	4-speed wide-ratio manual standard, 4-speed close-ratio manual and 3-speed automatic optional
Wheelbase	98 inches
Overall width	69 inches
Overall height	47.5 inches
Overall length	182.5 inches
Track, front	58.7 inches
Track, rear	59.4 inches
Weight	3,400 pounds
Wheels	15x8 inches
Tires	F70x15 bias ply
Front suspension	independent unequal length wishbones and coil springs, anti-sway bar, telescopic shock absorbers
Rear suspension	independent radius arms, transverse leaf spring, half shafts acting as upper locating members, lower transverse rods, telescopic shock absorbers
Steering	recirculating ball
Brakes	4-wheel disc, 4-piston calipers, 11.75-inch rotors front and rear, 461.2 square inches swept area.
0 to 60 mph	6.0 seconds (350/330 w/ 3.70:1 axle and 4-speed manual transmission), 5.3 seconds (454/425 w/ 3.36:1 axle and 4-speed manual transmission)
Standing 1/4-mile	14.57 seconds @ 100.55 mph (350/330 w/ 3.70:1 axle and 4-speed manual transmission), 13.8 seconds @ 104.65 mph (454/425 w/ 3.36:1 axle and 4-speed manual transmission)
Top speed	137 mph (350/330 w/ 3.70:1 axle and 4-speed manual transmission), 152 mph (454/425 w/ 3.36:1 axle and 4-speed manual transmission)

The center console and center instrument housing were originally black regardless of interior color. A stainless steel trim tag in the doorjamb on the left side contains a code for exterior paint color, interior color, and seat material, plus the date the body was assembled.

The 454 engine compartment is crowded indeed. As a result, simple maintenance, such as changing spark plugs, can be quite difficult, especially when the car is equipped with air conditioning.

All C3s, even the earlier ones, make great drivers. However, the early cars are definitely noisier and stiffer riding compared with later ones. A 1971 equipped with the base engine is reasonably quick. For brutal acceleration, go for the optional LT1 or one of the two available big-block engines.

1971 Corvette Major Options

		Quantity	Price
A31	Power windows	6,192	$79
A85	Custom shoulder harness	677	$42
C07	Auxiliary hardtop	2,619	$274
C08	Auxiliary hardtop vinyl trim	832	$63
C50	Rear window defroster	1,598	$42
C60	Air conditioning	11,481	$459
J50	Vacuum power brakes	13,558	$47
LS5	454/365-horsepower engine	5,079	$295
LS6	454/425-horsepower engine	188	$1,221
LT1	350/330-horsepower Engine	1,949	$483
M21	4-speed close-ratio manual transmission	2,387	no charge
M22	4-speed heavy-duty manual transmission	130	$100
M40	Turbo Hydra-Matic transmission	10,060	no charge (small-block), $100 (LS5 or LS6)
N37	Tilt & Telescopic steering column	8,130	$84.30
N40	Power steering	17,904	$115.90
PT7	F70-15 white stripe nylon tires	6,711	$28
PU9	F70-15 white letter nylon tires	12,449	$42
PO2	Deluxe wheel trim covers	3,007	$63
T60	Heavy-duty battery	1,455	$15.80
U69	AM-FM radio	21,509	$178
U79	Stereo equipment	3,431	$283
ZQ1	Rear-axle selection	2,395	$13
ZR1	350/330-horsepower engine, special*	8	$1,010
ZR2	454/425-horsepower engine, special*	12	$1,747
	Leather interior trim	2,602	$158

*Options ZR1 and ZR2 are both road-racing packages. The ZR1 package includes an LT1 engine, and the ZR2 package includes an LS6 engine. Both packages also include stiffer front and rear springs, heavy-duty shock absorbers, a special Harrison aluminum radiator (part number 3007436), and a heavy-duty brake package. The brake package includes twin-pin front calipers, an extra support for each front caliper, a proportioning valve, and metallic brake pads. N40 power steering, A31 power windows, PO2 wheel covers, C50 rear window defroster, and C60 air conditioning could not be ordered with the ZR1 package. The ZR1 package could only be ordered with an M22 4-speed transmission, while the ZR2 could be ordered with either an M22 or an M40 automatic.

The emissions components in a large majority of vintage Corvettes were removed many years ago. If you are not concerned with total originality and do not live in a state where the absence of such equipment may prevent you from registering the car, then you need not worry about it. If, however, you intend to seriously show the car or your state requires it, then you will need to locate and purchase the missing parts. Keep in mind that they can be quite hard to find and very expensive. For example, a complete, correct AIR system typically sells for about $1,500.

The optional LS6 454 turned the increasingly civilized Corvette into a brutal beast. Only 188 were built in 1971, the only year the potent engine was offered in Corvette. Those that survive are highly prized by collectors.

If you are considering purchasing a 1971 LS6, keep in mind that many of the parts unique to this potent engine are difficult to locate and expensive when they are found. Rare components include the Holley carburetor, aluminum cylinder heads, and transistor ignition setup.

Problems with the vacuum-actuated wiper door cover and headlamp housings are common. All of the relevant components, including the vacuum motor shown here, are available, but tracking down and fixing problems in the system can be time consuming.

What They Said in 1971

330 horses and damn close to 140 miles per hour—a beautiful bundle of eminently controllable brutality. The drawbacks are those of most sports cars, with savage fuel consumption thrown in, but sports cars have never been for the practically-minded. —*Sports Car World,* May 1971

I Bought a 1971 Corvette

I own two 1970 coupes and a 1972 convertible. I restored them to perfection and was looking for a 1971 restoration candidate. The 1971 I bought was a good, solid car that needed cosmetics, a front-end rebuild, and an engine rebuild. A lot of the dated parts under the hood were wrong, and the interior was incorrect, with the wrong type of carpeting and leather seats instead of vinyl. I enjoy going through the restoration process, making my cars look exactly as they did when they left the factory. I also like driving them, and C3s are very enjoyable to drive when they are correctly restored. —Lee Mantel

Regular AM-FM radio and AM-FM stereo were both extra-cost options in 1971, and both often do not work or do not work well. Make sure the problem is not in the speakers or the amplifier before sending the radio out for repairs.

The heavy-duty M22 four-speed, which went into only 130 Corvettes in 1971, has a distinct whine. Much more common M20 and M21 four-speeds should be quiet when the car is moving.

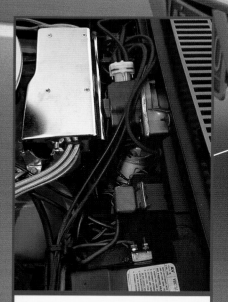

The windshield wiper motor is electric, while the washer pump is vacuum powered. Besides sending cleaning fluid to the windshield, the pump also routed it to the headlamps. It's common for the washer pump to not work, but rebuild kits are available.

Original or correct reproduction tires look wonderful and are important if you intend to show the car in National Corvette Restorers Society or other serious events, but modern radials handle and ride much better.

Fuel tank rust is a fairly common problem. Because of Corvette's unusual top-fill setup, you can simply look directly into the tank to see if the bottom of the inside is rusty.

All 1971 Corvettes came with a blue certification label glued toward the top of the rear portion of the driver-side door. It contains the car's serial number as well as the month and year the car was assembled.

Though seen with some frequency, luggage racks were never a factory option for Corvette. This particular style rack was, however, a Chevrolet dealer accessory. Other designs were offered in the aftermarket. If you don't like the rack, keep in mind that removal will necessitate repairing the holes and repainting the rear deck.

Though horsepower figures are considerably lower than in previous years, a change in the way the power was measured was partly to blame. Actual over-the-road performance for 1972s changed little from the previous year.

Reduction in engine compression ratios and accompanying decline in horsepower initiated in 1970 continued in 1972. Chevrolet also changed the way in which it quoted horsepower figures, going from SAE gross to SAE net. The former measured power at the flywheel on a test stand, while the latter measured it at the wheels with all engine accessories installed. Stingrays equipped with the optional LT1 small-block or LS5 big-block were still very quick but not quite as fast as in the previous two years.

This was the final year for a number of features, and for that reason, it is a little more popular than 1971 with some collectors. Making their final appearance were front and rear chrome bumpers, a Corvette tradition since the beginning in 1953. It was also the final appearance for the vacuum-operated door concealing the car's windshield wipers and for the egg-crate side fender vents and front-grille treatment.

Putting the evolutionary changes aside, 1972 was not too different from the cars that immediately preceded it or the ones that immediately followed it. Coupes were reasonably tight, free of rattles, and weather resistant. Many years after they were built, the T-tops are prone to leaking water, but new weatherstrips and some adjustments remedy that.

Convertibles comprised slightly less than 25 percent of production but are considerably more popular with collectors today. Lacking the extra rigidity imparted by the coupe's central roof member, convertibles have noticeably more shimmy and rattle on bumpy roads. As you would expect, they are also susceptible to wind noise and some water leakage. Both can usually be with new convertible top seals and careful adjustment of the top frame and side windows. A removable hardtop was optional, and people like to have these, but in reality, they are rarely used. The hardtop is heavy and unwieldy, so removing and installing it requires two able-bodied people.

Reflecting the evolution of buyers' expectations, nearly 75 percent of 1972 Corvettes were ordered with air conditioning. Other luxury features, such as power steering, power brakes, Tilt & Telescopic steering column, and stereo radio, were also ordered in greater numbers than ever

before. This makes low-option, stripped-down 1972s rather unusual and generally less desirable than well-equipped examples, despite the fact that they are rarer. Adding to their desirability, better-optioned cars are also markedly more enjoyable to drive today, as we are all accustomed to air conditioning and other niceties.

The rarest of all 1972s came with option ZR1. This was essentially a road-racing package that included LT1 engine; heavy-duty, close-ratio four-speed transmission; heavy-duty power brakes; special springs, shocks, and sway bars; transistor ignition; and an oversize aluminum radiator. Only 20 cars were built with option ZR1, and the few that survive are highly coveted. Well-documented examples fetch in excess of $100,000.

As with other C3s, when considering a 1972 for purchase, be on the lookout for evidence of severe body damage and substandard repairs. You should be able to spot extensive damage and shoddy repairs by examining the underside of the body. Use a strong light, and look up in the wheelwells, up underneath the area where the front fenders meet the cowl, and underneath the front of the nose in the area of the headlamps. The underside of all body panels should be smooth, unpainted, and dark gray in color. Adjacent panels should be secured by a fiberglass bonding strip glued to their underside.

Another common problem with C3s is rust. The fiberglass body is immune, but the steel chassis, radiator support, rear trailing arms, and body substructure are not. Particularly troublesome areas include the steel framework surrounding the windshield and the chassis side rails beneath the doors.

While evaluating structural integrity and cosmetics is important, it is also important that you investigate the function of all components and systems. Run the car and listen to the engine for any abnormal noises. Monitor the coolant temperature and oil pressure gauges. If you are able and the owner is willing, do a compression check of the engine and measure vacuum with a gauge. Look at the backside of the wheels for evidence of brake fluid leakage. Look at the underside of the car for evidence of other fluid leaks. Fluid leaks are commonly seen at the steering box's pitman shaft seal, differential pinion seal, engine-rear main seal, and power steering valve and hydraulic ram. Make sure all electrical components work. Drive the car and listen for groans, whines, and other revealing noises in the transmission and differential.

1972 Corvette Ratings

Model Comfort/Amenities	***
Reliability ****	
Collectibility	*****
Parts/Service Availability	****
Est. Annual Maintenance Costs	$450

1972 Corvette Replacement Costs for Common Parts

Convertible top w/ pads and straps	$210
Windshield (correct reproduction)	$450
Seat upholstery (pair, correct vinyl)	$250
Seat upholstery (pair, correct leather)	$460
Carpet	$275
Door panels (pair, correct reproduction w/out any trim)	$210
Hood (correct press-molded reproduction)	$900
Front fender (correct press-molded reproduction)	$300
Wheel	$125
Headlamp assembly (including cup, ring, adjusters, bezel mount kit, and bulb)	$50
Taillamp housing and lens	$110
Exhaust system	$275
Shock absorber	$75
Front wheel bearing	$15
Front springs (pair)	$100
Brake master cylinder (functional replacement)	$100
Brake caliper (stainless steel sleeved)	$100
Radiator (correct dated reproduction for small-block)	$800
Radiator support	$350
Water pump	$75 (rebuilt original)
Ignition shielding	$360
Cylinder head (pair)	$300 (small-block rebuildable originals)
Rear leaf spring (functional replacement)	$110
Complete tune-up kit (ignition points, condenser, plugs, distributor cap, rotor, ignition wires)	$60
Fuel tank	$200

The C3 Corvette interior can be confining for some, but most people get used to it quickly. This beautifully preserved original car has the custom interior trim option. Included in the option package were plusher carpeting, leather seat covers, simulated wood trim on the center console and door panels, and a strip of carpet along the bottom of the door panels.

1972 Corvette Specifications

Base price (new)	$5,533 (coupe)
	$5,296 (convertible)
Production	20,496 (coupe)
	6,508 (convertible)
Engine	V-8
Bore x stroke (small-block, inches)	4x3.48
Displacement (small-block)	350-ci
Bore x stroke (big-block, inches)	4.25x4
Displacement (big-block)	454-ci
Compression ratio	8.5:1 (base engine)
Horsepower	200 (base engine)
Transmission	4-speed wide-ratio manual standard, 4-speed close-ratio manual and 3-speed automatic optional
Wheelbase	98 inches
Overall width	69 inches
Overall height	47.5 inches
Overall length	182.5 inches
Track, front	58.7 inches
Track, rear	59.4 inches
Weight	3,400 pounds
Wheels	15x8 inches
Tires	F70x15 bias ply
Front suspension	independent unequal length wishbones and coil springs, anti-sway bar, telescopic shock absorbers
Rear suspension	independent radius arms, transverse leaf spring, half shafts acting as upper locating members, lower transverse rods, telescopic shock absorbers
Steering	recirculating ball
Brakes	4-wheel disc, 4-piston calipers, 11.75-inch rotors front and rear, 461.2 square inches swept area
0 to 60 mph	8.9 seconds (350/200 w/ 3.36:1 axle and automatic transmission), 5.8 seconds (454/270 w/ 3.08:1 axle and automatic transmission)
Standing 1/4-mile	15.644 seconds @ 89.64 mph (350/200 w/ 3.36:1 axle and automatic transmission), 14.24 seconds @ 100.4 mph (454/270 w/ 3.08:1 axle and automatic transmission)
Top speed	125 mph (350/200 w/ 3.36:1 axle and automatic transmission), 142 mph (454/270 w/ 3.08:1 axle and automatic transmission)

1972 Corvette Major Options

		Quantity	Price
AV3	3-point seatbelts	17,693	
A31	Power windows	9,495	$85.35
A85	Deluxe shoulder harness	749	$42.15
C07	Auxiliary hardtop	2,646	$273.85
C08	Auxiliary hardtop vinyl trim	811	$158.00
C50	Rear window defroster	2,221	$42.15
C60	Air conditioning	17,011	$464.50
F41	Special suspension	20	(included w/ ZR1 option package)
J50	Vacuum power brakes	18,770	$47.40
J56	Heavy-duty brakes	20	(included w/ ZR1 option package)
K19	Air injection reactor	3,912	no charge
LS5	454/270-horsepower engine	3,913	$294.90
LT1	350/255-horsepower engine	1,741	$483.45
M21	4-speed close-ratio manual transmission	1,638	no charge
M22	4-speed heavy-duty manual transmission	20	(included w/ ZR1 option package)
M40	Turbo Hydra-Matic transmission	14,543	no charge (small-block), $100.35 (LS5)
NB2	Exhaust emission control	1,766	no charge
N37	Tilt & Telescopic steering column	12,992	$84.30
N40	Power steering	23,794	$115.90
PT1	F70-15 blackwall tires	3,716	no charge
PT7	F70-15 white stripe nylon tires	6,666	$30.35
PU9	F70-15 white letter nylon tires	16,623	$43.65
PO2	Deluxe wheel trim covers	3,593	$63.20
T60	Heavy-duty battery	2,969	$15.80
UL5	Radio delete	292	no charge
U69	AM-FM radio	26,669	$178
U79	Stereo equipment	5,832	$283.35
YF5	California emissions	1,967	$15.80
ZR1	350/255-horsepower engine, special**	20	$1,010.05
ZR5	3-point shoulder belts	2	no charge
ZR7	Factory delivery	16	no charge
ZV1	Statement of origin	135	no charge
ZW4	4-speed wide-ratio manual transmission	10,804	no charge

**Option ZR1 is a road-racing package that includes an LT1 engine, stiffer front and rear springs, heavy-duty shock absorbers, a special Harrison aluminum radiator (part number 3007436), an M22 4-speed transmission, and a heavy-duty brake package. The brake package includes twin-pin front calipers, an extra support for each front caliper, a proportioning valve, and metallic brake pads. N40 power steering, A31 power windows, PO2 wheel covers, C50 rear window defroster, and C60 air conditioning could not be ordered with the ZR1 package. In 1972 (but not in 1970 or 1971), ZR1-equipped cars do not have a fan shroud.

The federally required vehicle emissions control information decal was different depending on which engine came in the car. The presence of an original sticker can help document which engine came in the car, but a reproduction sticker tells you nothing. The sticker was located on the driver-side cowl behind the brake master cylinder.

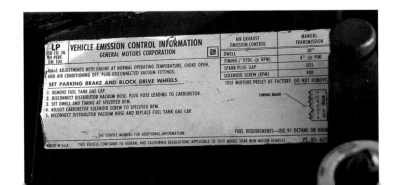

All Corvette rally wheels are stamped with a date code, manufacturer's logo, and size code on the front face. Original Corvette wheels have the code "AZ" stamped adjacent to the valve stem hole.

Aluminum intake manifold and valve covers immediately differentiate the optional LT1 engine from the base small-block. This unrestored, magnificently preserved engine compartment is a collector's dream.

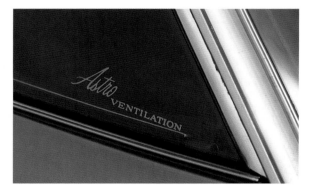

Astro Ventilation referred to the largely inadequate interior ventilation system utilized through 1974. By itself, the system really didn't move enough air through the cockpit to keep passengers comfortable in the heat of summer. Both side windows came with "Astro Ventilation" silk-screened in white letters.

What They Said in 1972

Some of the ponies are missing from the 1972 Corvette Stingray, but the prestige is still there! You know you are driving a very special car when the kids in the car wash argue over who is to drive it through! The Corvette Stingray still elicits this excitement among the "now" generation, but the 1972 version is a small step backward for the nineteen-year-old sports car from Chevrolet. —*Road Test*, May 1972

I Bought a 1972 Corvette

My brother bought a 1972 as an almost-new car in 1973. I bought it from him in 1978. It has 155,000 miles on the clock and has been a very reliable and enjoyable car. I had a valve job done at 145,000 miles, because it was blowing blue smoke out the tailpipe from oil getting past the valve seals. I also restored the power steering and resealed the transmission and rear end to stop all of the leaks that developed over the years. It still has the original paint and interior, both of which look a little tired in some spots, but we think this adds a welcome patina to the car. —Andrew Sacks

Vacuum headlamp assemblies often don't work properly and can be somewhat confusing to diagnose. The problem is usually vacuum related—a leak, incorrectly connected lines, or a faulty component. Sometimes mechanical issues, such as binding in the linkage that moves the door up and down, is also a factor.

Contrary to what many people assume, imperfections are sometimes desirable when it comes to vintage Corvettes. If you look closely at the factory-original paint stripes on this 1972 LT1 hood, you see that they are irregular in width, especially beneath the "T," where a narrower section meets a slightly wider one. This resulted from the stencil the factory used and is preferable to perfect stripes, which usually result in a point deduction at a serious Corvette show.

All big-block cars came with heavy, cast steel caps retaining half shaft U-joints to the differential side yokes. This is one example of the numerous features unique to big blocks that you should look for when evaluating one for purchase.

All radio-equipped Corvettes came with chrome-plated ignition shielding. Only big blocks came with the stainless steel braided spark plug wires seen here. The shielding is often missing but is being reproduced.

Examination of individual components can reveal a lot about how a car has been treated over the years. This alternator has its original wire loom bracket, correct pulley and fan, and correct fasteners. Though not visible in this photo, it also has the correct part number and date code for the car. This is the kind of authenticity and detail that separates mediocre cars from real gems.

A Corvette will still run and drive without various non-essential underhood components, such as the emissions equipment, but the absence of these will reduce value for most enthusiasts. Take stock of what is missing or incorrect, and consider this when deciding how much you are willing to pay for a prospective purchase.

All C3 Corvettes utilize an inner and an outer wheel bearing on each side in the rear. Because there is no easy way to grease these bearings, they are often neglected and prone to failure after many years and miles of use. Squealing, whining, or groaning noises from the wheel assembly and excessive side-to-side or up-and-down play in the rear-wheel spindle are strong indications of bearing trouble.

The Corvette's transformation from a brutal muscle car into a more-refined grand touring machine was well underway by 1973. Though not as fast as earlier big-block models, this 454-equipped convertible was still among the fastest production cars made in 1973. This particular example has traveled only 3,900 miles since new and is one of the best original examples to be found anywhere.

Corvette's transformation from a brutish musclecar to a more-refined grand touring machine continued in 1973. All of the basic convenience and luxury features that are standard on nearly every car made today were still optional, but the majority of Corvettes were ordered with them. For example, more than 70 percent had air conditioning, and more than 91 percent had power steering. That means today's 1973 Corvette buyer can enjoy a car that is very easy to drive on a regular basis.

Adding to the car's ease of use today is the fact that the available engines were de-tuned, compared to powerplants from prior years. In 1973, the base 350 engine developed only 190 horsepower, while the optional 350, called L82, gave 250 horsepower. Surprisingly, the 454 big-block was still offered. It was rated at a relatively modest 275 horsepower. All of these engines feature maintenance-free hydraulic lifter camshafts and low compression ratios. It was the first time in Corvette history that a solid-lifter engine was not offered.

The raw acceleration that characterized earlier Corvettes isn't there, but 1973 models willingly run on 91-octane pump gas without pinging. Also, they are less likely to run hot and more likely to pass an emissions test in those locales that require it.

Besides the continuing movement toward greater luxury, which reflected changes in the buying-public's tastes and expectations, certain characteristics of 1973 Corvettes were shaped by increasingly stringent governmental intervention, namely federal safety and emissions regulations. For example, the chrome-plated front bumper, a Corvette staple since its 1953 beginning, yielded to an energy-absorbing bumper that complied with federal 5 mile per hour impact requirements. An injection-molded, body-color urethane cover went over the impact structure. To further improve occupant safety, steel impact beams were required in each door.

While the added safety features are certainly welcome, an undesirable byproduct of these, as well as of the increasing array of emissions control apparatus, was increased chassis weight. Combined with reduced horsepower, the additional

weight further diminished Corvette's speed and acceleration numbers. Of course, these same forces impacted all cars of the era, and, therefore, all offered decreased performance.

Though brute horsepower and neck-snapping acceleration were largely a thing of the past by 1973, many of the quality-control problems that plagued early C3s were also disappearing. Newly designed body-mount cushions better isolated occupants from road noise and vibration. Interior noise was also noticeably reduced through the addition of a sprayed-on, asphalt-based insulation; added insulation under the dash; and an insulating blanket under the hood. Like the safety features and emissions equipment, this added more weight, but it also enhanced the driving experience.

The vacuum-operated windshield wiper door introduced in 1968 was eliminated for 1973. The wipers were instead concealed by a revised hood that extended farther back toward the windshield. A neat feature of the new hood was a cold-air duct system that took in outside air from the base of the windshield and fed it into the carburetor via a solenoid-actuated valve during hard acceleration.

Despite their numerous refinements and improvements, 1973 Corvettes still suffer from a number of common problems. Rust in the chassis, windshield frame, and radiator support is something to watch out for. Leaking brake calipers are another common malady. New seals typically won't solve this problem for long, because it is due to corrosion in the cylinder bores that leads to rapid failure of new seals. The long-term solution is to install stainless steel, sleeved calipers if they haven't already been installed.

Body damage and poor fiberglass repairs are also something to look for when inspecting a car for purchase. Examine the underside of body panels, which should be dark gray in color and free from cracks, patches, or other evidence of collision damage. Avoid cars that have aftermarket one-piece noses. Installing such a nose to fix front-end body damage is relatively cheap and easy, but doing so deviates from the car's original construction and seriously diminishes its value to many people.

As with any year Corvette, originality of major components such as the engine block is important to many enthusiasts. There is nothing wrong with buying a car with the engine and other major components replaced if factory authenticity is not important to you, but make sure that you pay a price that is consistent with the lack of originality.

1973 Corvette Ratings

Model Comfort/Amenities	****
Reliability	****
Collectibility	****
Parts/Service Availability	****
Est. Annual Maintenance Costs	$450

1973 Corvette Replacement Costs

Convertible top w/pads and straps	$210
Windshield (correct reproduction)	$450
Seat upholstery (pair, correct vinyl)	$250
Seat upholstery (pair, correct leather)	$460
Carpet	$275
Door panels (pair, correct reproduction w/out any trim)	$210
Hood (correct press-molded reproduction)	$900
Front fender (correct press-molded reproduction)	$300
Wheel	$125
Headlamp assembly (including cup, ring, adjusters, bezel mount kit, and bulb)	$50
Taillamp housing and lens	$110
Exhaust system	$275
Shock absorber	$75
Front wheel bearing	$15
Front springs (pair)	$100
Brake master cylinder (functional replacement)	$100
Brake caliper (stainless steel sleeved)	$100
Radiator (correct dated reproduction for small-block)	$800
Radiator support	$350
Water pump, rebuilt original	$75
Ignition shielding	$360
Cylinder head (pair, small-block rebuildable originals)	$300
Rear leaf spring (functional replacement)	$110
Complete tune-up kit (ignition points, condenser, plugs, distributor cap, rotor, ignition wires)	$60
Fuel tank	$200

1973 Corvette Specifications

Base price (new)	$5,561.50 (coupe)
	$5,398.50 (convertible)
Production	25,521 (coupe)
	4,943 (convertible)
Engine	V-8
Bore x stroke (small-block, inches)	4x3.48
Displacement (small-block)	350-ci
Bore x stroke (big-block, inches)	4.25x4
Displacement (big-block)	454-ci
Compression ratio	8.25:1 (base engine)
Horsepower	190 (base engine)
Transmission	4-speed wide-ratio manual standard, 4-speed close-ratio manual and 3-speed automatic optional
Wheelbase	98 inches
Overall width	69 inches
Overall height	47.7 inches
Overall length	184.7 inches
Track, front	58.7 inches
Track, rear	59.5 inches
Weight	3,585 pounds
Wheels	15x8 inches
Tires	GR70x15 radials
Front suspension	independent unequal length wishbones and coil springs, anti-sway bar, telescopic shock absorbers
Rear suspension	independent radius arms, transverse leaf spring, anti-sway bar half shafts acting as upper locating members, lower transverse rods, telescopic shock absorbers
Steering	recirculating ball
Brakes	4-wheel disc, 4-piston calipers, 11.75-inch rotors front and rear, 461.2 square inches swept area
0 to 60 mph	6.7 seconds (350/250 w/ 3.70:1 axle and 4-speed manual transmission), 6.4 seconds (454/275 w/ 3.08:1 axle and automatic transmission)
Standing 1/4[fractionfont]-mile	15.1 seconds @ 95.4 mph (350/250 w/ 3.70:1 axle and 4-speed manual transmission), 14.7 seconds @ 97.2 mph (454/275 w/ 3.08:1 axle and automatic transmission)
Top speed	117 mph (350/250 w/ 3.70:1 axle and 4-speed manual transmission), 142 mph (454/275 w/ 3.08:1 axle and automatic transmission)

Radial tires were factory installed on Corvettes beginning in 1973. They dramatically improved both handling and ride quality.

Aluminum wheels were supposed to be optional in 1973, but porosity problems reportedly led to their cancellation. According to published production figures, only four cars were built with them before the option was discontinued. All remaining 1973s came with standard center caps and trim rings on rally rims, or with optional PO2 Deluxe Wheel Covers.

If you are looking for a factory-correct car, familiarize yourself with the difficulty and cost involved in procuring any parts that are not correct on the car you are considering. A correctly dated and numbered alternator for this car is relatively easy to find and will cost perhaps $250 properly restored and detailed. A correctly dated and numbered carburetor for this same car is extremely difficult to find and can easily set you back $800 or more for a pristine example.

Vintage Corvettes tend to run too hot, especially big blocks equipped with air conditioning. Make sure that the many seals designed to force air through the radiator, rather than around it, are in place.

1973 Corvette Major Options

		Quantity	Price
A31	Power windows	14,024	$83
A85	Deluxe shoulder harness	788	$41
C07	Auxiliary hardtop	1,328	$267
C08	Auxiliary hardtop vinyl trim	323	$62
C50	Rear window defroster	4,412	$41
C60	Air conditioning	21,578	$452
J50	Vacuum power brakes	24,168	$46
LS4	454/275-horsepower engine	4,412	$250
L48	350/190-horsepower engine	20,342	standard
L82	350/250-horsepower engine	5,710	$299
M20	Standard 4-speed manual transmission	8,833	no charge
M21	4-speed close-ratio manual transmission	3,704	no charge
M40	Turbo Hydra-Matic transmission	17,927	no charge (small-block) $97 (LS4 or L82)
N37	Tilt & Telescopic steering column	17,949	$82
N40	Power steering	27,872	$113
PO2	Deluxe wheel trim covers	1,739	$62
QRM	GR70-15 white stripe radial tires	19,903	$32
QRN	GR70-15 blackwall radial tires	6,020	no charge
QRZ	GR70-15 white letter radial tires	4,541	$45
T60	Heavy-duty battery	4,912	$15
U58	AM-FM stereo radio	12,482	$276
U69	AM-FM radio	17,598	$173
UF1	Map light	8,186	$5
UL5	Radio delete	384	no charge
YF5	California emissions	3,008	$15
YJ8	Aluminum wheels	4	$175
	Rear-axle ratio selection	1,791	$12
	Custom interior w/ leather trim	13,434	$154

Early Corvette air conditioning systems do an excellent job of cooling when they are working properly. Unfortunately, they frequently do not work at all. Diagnosing and repairing air conditioning problems is usually quite expensive. Sellers often say that the system just needs a charge, but if it was that simple, why didn't they get it done before putting the car up for sale?

The 1973 Corvette was the only year with urethane front and chrome-plated rear bumpers. Some people like the look and appreciate the uniqueness of this, while others prefer chrome all around, as seen earlier, or urethane all around, as seen later.

Don't forget to make sure the car's original jack, lug wrench, and spare tire are present. The jack and lug wrench should be in the storage compartment behind the seats, and the spare should be in a fiberglass housing underneath the rear and between the mufflers.

All soft-trim items and most other parts for 1973 interiors are readily available but their cost can add up quickly. It is often difficult to replace only some items because remaining items look shabby in comparison to the new ones.

What They Said in 1973

Zora Arkus-Duntov reckons the new Corvette to be the best ever, and after exhaustive testing of four different models, we're inclined to agree.
—*Car and Driver*, December 1972

I Bought a 1973 Corvette

I always liked the fact that 1973 Corvettes have the rubber bumper in the front and chrome bumpers in the back. That look was for one year only and makes 1973s unique. I found my car through word of mouth and brought along some friends from my club to help me look at it. The car was well cared for but did need new paint and some interior work. I paid a fair price for it and have been very happy so far. Even with the T-tops off, it gets quite hot on the inside in the summer, so air conditioning really is a must if you're going to drive a coupe in the hot summer months. —Darren Wagner

1973 Garage Watch

Though fiberglass does not rust, there is still plenty of steel on a C3 Corvette that can. One area that is particularly prone to corrosion is the steel frame surrounding the windshield. Though interior trim covers much of this frame, you can still see small segments of corrosion where the VIN tag is riveted and along the base.

Early Corvette urethane bumpers don't usually hold up very well over time. If cracks or crazing are evident through the paint, plan on replacing the bumper cover rather than trying to repair it. If the cover is sound but the paint is a slightly different shade, don't assume it indicates some sort of damage occurred. Urethane bumper covers are typically a slightly different color from the rest of the car.

Nearly every major underhood component has a part number and date code. If technical correctness and originality are important to you, familiarize yourself with the locations of these numbers and codes, and check them when evaluating a car for purchase. A generally accepted rule of thumb is that the manufacturing date for each component should precede the final assembly date of the car by no more than six months.

After 30 years and a lot of miles, the positraction unit in the differential can act up. The most common indication of a problem is a clunking or chattering sound, often accompanied by a bang you can feel in the seat of your pants, when the car is turning. This problem is usually worse when the car has been driven a while and the positraction fluid is hot.

Original Corvette radios often don't play well or don't play at all. The problem is as likely to be a bad antenna connection or defective speakers as a broken radio.

Always confirm the presence of an original serial number tag on any car you are considering for purchase. All C3s came with a tag riveted to the driver-side windshield pillar.z

All C3 Corvettes came with a trim tag riveted to the driver-side door's hinge pillar. The tag contains codes for original exterior and interior colors, original seat material, and body assembly date. Make sure this tag is present, and check whether the colors and seat material have been changed. Even if it's not important to you, changes usually diminish the value of the car and should be taken into consideration when negotiating a price.

In 1974, buyers still had a lot of different choices when it came to options for their Corvette, and the majority loaded up on air conditioning, full power, and other niceties. Though brutally powerful engines were a thing of the past, L82- or LS4-optioned cars were still pretty quick in the context of the time period.

Corvette's transition away from a musclecar toward a more rounded grand touring sports car continued in 1974. This resulted from both evolving expectations among buyers as well as changes mandated by increasingly stringent federal safety and emissions regulations.

The impact-absorbing, urethane-covered front bumper system introduced in 1973 was utilized for the rear bumper as well beginning in 1974. A body-colored urethane skin with a seam in the middle covered an aluminum impact bar mounted to the chassis with two telescopic energy absorbers.

The rear bumper cover used in 1975 and later was similar, but it did not have a vertical seam in the middle. Also, in 1974 the cover had provisions for two vertical license plate lamps, one on each side of the plate, while later covers had a single lamp above the plate. The correct 1974 cover was long ago discontinued by Chevrolet and is not currently being reproduced, so most 1974 owners in need of a new one simply install the later design, which functions properly and is readily available. If you are planning to buy a 1974 and enter it in NCRS shows or other high-level events, try to find one with a good rear bumper.

Corvettes were slightly more comfortable in 1974 for several reasons. A deeper recess in the floor yielded more foot room. Distribution of air conditioned air was improved with revised ducting. Standard shoulder belts for the coupe were unified into a single assembly with the lapbelt. Shoulder belts remained optional for convertibles, however, and those continued to be separate from the lapbelts. In accordance with new governmental requirements, seatbelts had an interlock that prevented the engine from starting unless the belts were buckled.

Stricter California noise regulations induced Chevrolet to rethink Corvette's exhaust system. Resonators were added to each tailpipe forward of the muffler, resulting in not only a quieter exhaust note outside but also a quieter interior for passengers. Another subtle but welcome change to the interior was a widening of the inside rearview mirror from 8 to 10 inches for better rearward visibility.

A new wiring harness introduced in 1974 was said to be more reliable and easier to repair. However, previously used harnesses were not especially problematic or difficult to repair. Regardless, excellent reproduction harnesses are readily available, and if you encounter an aged harness that has multiple splices and repairs, your best course of action is to replace it with a new one.

The chronic engine-heat control problem common to earlier Corvettes, especially those fitted with big-block engines, was reduced a great deal by 1974. This is commendable since increasingly crowded engine compartments seen in the early and mid-1970s impaired the flow of air around the engine, thus making it more difficult to cool them. Detuned engines with lower compression ratios and milder cam profiles phased in beginning in the early 1970s generally ran cooler. To further alleviate the problem, a new radiator design was adopted for 1974. It was particularly effective at low road speeds when airflow through the radiator was not good.

Problems commonly found in many C3s, including chassis, windshield frame, and radiator-support rust; leaking brake calipers; vacuum system leaks; radio and clock malfunctions; worn positraction units; and broken parking brake systems are also likely to be found in 1974 models.

All of these common problems and virtually anything else that is wrong with a 1974 can be fixed, as most parts are readily available. It simply distills down to a matter of time and money, and this is where later C3s sometimes run into a vexing problem. It costs the same to fix most problems and do most restoration projects, whether your car is a more-valuable early C3 or a less-valuable later one. And, given that the chassis design used through 1982 was first introduced in 1963, any sort of chassis-related work entails the same labor and parts for all Corvettes going back to 1963.

An appealing aspect of most 1974 (1974 to 1977 in particular, and 1978 to 1982 to a slightly lesser extent) Corvettes is their relative affordability. In a sense, however, this becomes a liability, because the cost to do any sort of serious restoration work will often exceed the total value of the car after the work is completed. If this is a concern to you, you are far better off paying more up front for a car that needs little or no work.

Corvette's interior benefited from numerous minor revisions in 1974, but the overall appearance was essentially unchanged from the previous year. Shown here is the Custom Interior Trim option, which included leather seat covers, plusher carpeting, a carpet strip on the door panels, and faux wood trim on the door panels and center console.

1974 Corvette Ratings

Model Comfort/Amenities	****
Reliability	****
Collectibility	***(coupe) ****(convertible)
Parts/Service Availability	****
Est. Annual Maintenance Costs	$450

1974 Corvette Replacement Costs for Common Parts

Convertible top w/ pads and straps	$210
Windshield (correct reproduction)	$450
Seat upholstery (pair, correct vinyl)	$250
Seat upholstery (pair, correct leather)	$390
Carpet	$200
Door panels (pair, correct reproduction w/out any trim)	$210
Hood	$475
Front fender (correct press-molded reproduction)	$315
Wheel	$125
Headlamp assembly (including cup, ring, adjusters, bezel mount kit, and bulb)	$50
Taillamp lens	$55
Exhaust system	$275
Shock absorber	$75
Front wheel bearing	$15
Front springs (pair)	$100
Brake master cylinder (functional replacement)	$100
Brake caliper (stainless steel sleeved)	$100
Radiator (Harrison OEM type)	$475
Radiator support	$350
Water pump	$75 (rebuilt original)
Ignition shielding	$360
Cylinder head (pair)	$300 (small-block rebuildable originals)
Rear leaf spring (functional replacement)	$110
Complete tune-up kit (ignition points, condenser, plugs, distributor cap, rotor, ignition wires)	$60
Fuel tank	$200

1974 Corvette Specifications

Base price (new)	$6,001.50 (coupe)
	$5,765.50 (convertible)
Production	32,028 (coupe)
	5,474 (convertible)
Engine	V-8
Bore x stroke (small-block, inches)	4x3.48
Displacement (small-block)	350-ci
Bore x stroke (big-block, inches)	4.25x4
Displacement (big-block)	454-ci
Compression ratio	8.25:1 (base engine)
Horsepower	195 (base engine)
Transmission	4-speed wide-ratio manual standard, 4-speed close-ratio manual and 3-speed automatic optional
Wheelbase	98 inches
Overall width	69 inches
Overall height	48.1 inches
Overall length	185.5 inches
Track, front	58.7 inches
Track, rear	59.5 inches
Weight	3,542 pounds
Wheels	15x8 inches
Tires	GR70x15 radials
Front suspension	independent unequal length wishbones and coil springs, anti-sway bar, telescopic shock absorbers
Rear suspension	independent radius arms, transverse leaf spring, anti-sway bar half shafts acting as upper locating members, lower transverse rods, telescopic shock absorbers
Steering	recirculating ball
Brakes	4-wheel disc, 4-piston calipers, 11.75-inch rotors front and rear, 461.2 square inches swept area.
0 to 60 mph	8.9 seconds (350/195 w/ 3.55:1 axle and 4-speed manual transmission)
Standing 1/4-mile	15.6 seconds @ 92.3 mph (350/195 w/ 3.55:1 axle and 4-speed manual transmission)
Top speed	121 mph (350/195 w/ 3.55:1 axle and 4-speed manual transmission)

About two-thirds of all 1974s came with an automatic transmission. Fluid leaks are a common problem, especially with cars that are not driven regularly.

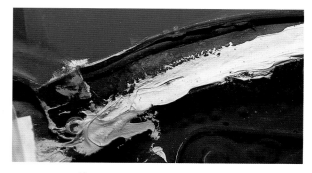

Thoroughly examining a vintage Corvette yields many clues about its condition. Why did someone smear some sort of sealant on the steel frame at the base of the windshield on this 1974? Probably because the frame is rotted through and was leaking water into the car's interior, a conclusion reinforced by the rust that is visible above the sealant.

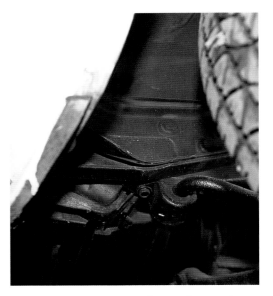

Compared with earlier Corvettes, the engine compartment was quite drab by 1974. A chrome ignition-shield cover was the only dress-up item used. Though not particularly powerful, the base engine was smooth running and extremely reliable when properly maintained.

Chassis damage resulting from a front-end collision is often readily apparent in the area of the frame where the front sway bar mounts. Look for kinks, tears, welds, and other abnormalities in these areas.

Vintage Corvette heating and air conditioning controls often do not function properly. The systems rely on both electrical and vacuum power. Go through all of the functions on the control wheels to determine what is and isn't working.

Maintenance is no easy chore with such a cramped engine compartment. This is yet another reason why previous owners were tempted to remove all non-essentials, such as emissions control equipment, and chuck it into the garbage.

1974 Corvette Major Options

		Quantity	Price
A31	Power windows	23,940	$86
A85	Deluxe shoulder harness	618	$41
C07	Auxiliary hardtop	2,612	$267
C08	Auxiliary hardtop w/ vinyl trim	367	$329
C50	Rear window defroster	9,322	$43
C60	Air conditioning	29,397	$467
FE7	Gymkhana suspension	1,905	$7
J50	Vacuum power brakes	33,306	$49
LS4	454/270-horsepower engine	3,494	$250
L82	350/250-horsepower engine	6,690	$299
M20	Standard 4-speed manual transmission	8,862	no charge
M21	4-speed close-ratio manual transmission	3,494	no charge
M40	Turbo Hydra-Matic transmission	25,146	no charge (small-block), $97 (early in year, LS4 or L82), $103 (later in year, LS4 or L82)
N37	Tilt & Telescopic steering column	27,700	$82
N41	Power steering	35,944	$117
QRM	GR70-15 white stripe radial tires	9,140	$32
QRN	GR70-15 blackwall radial tires	4,260	no charge
QRZ	GR70-15 white letter radial tires	24,102	$45
U05	Dual horns	5,258	$4
T60	Heavy-duty battery	4,912	$15
U58	AM-FM stereo radio	19,581	$276
U69	AM-FM radio	17,374	$173
UA1	Heavy-duty battery	9,169	$15
UF1	Map light	16,101	$5
UL5	Radio delete	547	no charge
YF5	California emissions		$20
Z07	Off-road suspension and brakes*	47	$400
	Rear-axle ratio selection	1,219	$12
	Custom interior w/ leather trim	19,959	$154

*Z07 off-road suspension and brakes is an option package available with LS4 or L82 only. It includes stiffer front and rear springs, heavy-duty shock absorbers, twin-pin front calipers, an extra support for each front caliper, a proportioning valve, and metallic brake pads.

What They Said in 1974

The Corvette marks its twenty-first year as one of the more remarkable automobiles this country has produced. —Road Test, February 1974

I Bought a 1974 Corvette

I bought my 1974 convertible new and still have it. There was a lot of talk back then in the buff books about a mid-engine Corvette coming next, but it never happened. I always thought it should be true to its heritage with a front-mounted V-8, and I'm glad it's still that way. I drove my car every day for about eleven years, accumulating the bulk of its 145,00 miles then. It has been extremely reliable mechanically, but the paint, seats, and a lot of the interior trim had problems, and, over time, all held up very poorly.

Clutch linkage consists of numerous moving parts between the pedal you push and the clutch pressure plate. All should be periodically lubricated, but few ever are. Sloppiness resulting from wear necessitates replacement of pertinent parts. The only really difficult items to replace are pedal shaft bushings or the pedal itself if the shaft is excessively worn.

Though still an extra-cost option, nearly 96 percent of all 1974s came with power steering. After many years of service, both the control valve and hydraulic actuator ram tend to leak some fluid.

A rear urethane bumper cover with vertical seam in the middle was used only in 1974 and is not currently being reproduced. For 1975s and later, seamless covers will fit but result in a point deduction at serious shows.

Check the function of all components, including the gauges, when evaluating a car for purchase. The 1974's were the first with an electronic oil pressure gauge. Like the electronic temperature gauge, it relied on a remote sending unit rather than direct measurement. A malfunctioning oil pressure or coolant temperature gauge may be due to a faulty gauge or a defective sending unit.

While the outer door skin is fiberglass, the inner housing is steel. As such, it is prone to corrosion and in extreme cases such as this, replacement of the entire door is warranted. Examine the bottom of both doors when inspecting a car for purchase.

The factory-installed glass in all C3s, including 1974s, contains a two-letter manufacturing date code. Here, the date code is TU, which translates to August 1973. Original glass is desirable to most collectors.

Look at the underside of any car you are considering, preferably while it is on a lift. The fluid and corrosion seen on the bottom of the power-brake booster was not apparent until the unit was viewed from below.

The last C3 convertibles were built in 1975, thus they hold a special allure for collectors. Many reference sources site rising safety concerns as one of the reasons why convertibles were discontinued, but the reality is that dwindling sales had a far greater impact than anything else. In 1965, 65 percent of Corvettes sold were convertibles. In 1970, the figure had dropped to 38 percent, and by 1975, it fell to a mere 12 percent.

A number of significant changes were made to Corvette for 1975, most in response to increasingly stringent emissions and safety regulations. For the first time since it received a V-8, in 1955, Corvette did not have a true dual exhaust. Instead, both engine pipes fed into a single catalytic converter, and two tailpipes exited the converter, creating the look of a dual exhaust. The catalytic converter was made from stainless steel and contained porous platinum- and palladium-coated pellets that catalyze the oxidation of exhaust emissions. Because of their semi-precious contents, converters are expensive to replace. More than one owner has simply gutted it when it no longer functioned, leaving the housing in place to create the illusion that it is still up and running. This is something to be concerned about if you live in a jurisdiction that will require your car to pass an emissions test.

Besides being the first year for a catalytic converter, 1975 was also the first year Corvette benefited from Chevrolet's high-energy ignition system (HEI). Besides reducing emissions, HEI's hotter spark provided faster startup, especially in wet weather, and aided all around performance.

Another emissions-reducing system initiated in 1975 was early fuel evaporation (EFE). EFE used a vacuum-actuated valve in the right exhaust manifold that rerouted exhaust gas through passages in the intake manifold and then out the left manifold. This accelerated engine warm-up and thus reduced the quantity of unburned fuel exiting the tailpipes.

Like most of the emissions-reducing systems added to Corvette beginning in the late 1960s, EFE was beneficial in that it reduced airborne pollution. The unwanted result of most of the new emissions equipment, however, was diminished performance and increased purchase, maintenance, and repair costs. For today's vintage-Corvette enthusiast interested in an emissions-era car, the difficulty—or challenge, depending on how one views it—is in locating missing parts, figuring out how it all works, and diagnosing and repairing problems. Of course, if you do not intend to show the car at a serious level, do not mind deviating from original configura-

tion, and do not have related legal concerns, it is a relatively straightforward matter to strip off most of the equipment and return to pre-emissions components.

Partly due to emissions issues and partly in response to evolving consumer expectations, a big-block engine was not offered in 1975. In fact, only one optional engine was available, the L82 350, and fewer than 7 percent of the cars built came with it.

Also, because of changes in the marketplace, 1975 was the final year for the convertible body style until it was reintroduced in 1986. Because of this, 1975 convertibles have always held a special allure for collectors. Today, there are still a fair number of very low-mileage examples around, because people went out of their way to preserve what they assumed would be desirable vehicles in the future. Those equipped with L82, four-speed, air conditioning, and lots of other options are the most desirable. Also very desirable from a collecting perspective are any of the 144 1975s equipped with option Z07, the offroad (i.e. racing) suspension and brake package.

Aside from very clean convertibles, cars optioned with Z07 and any super low-mileage, unrestored specimens, which are always in great demand, there is not much collector interest in 1975s. The potential for appreciation in value is therefore not great, and there is a decent chance of winding up with more money invested in the car than it's worth if it needs any significant level of restoration work. On the other hand, ordinary 1975s are quite inexpensive relative to most other year Corvettes and thus provide an opportunity to enjoy Corvette ownership for a relatively modest investment.

As with other C3s, rust in the chassis and related components is something to be on the lookout for. Rust in the windshield frame is another common problem to avoid if possible. If you intend to show your 1975 in high-level events such as NCRS shows, buy one that is as complete as possible, particularly in regard to emissions equipment.

The quality of C3 body panels improved steadily, and 1975s tend to be pretty good, though minor stress cracks, especially along body seams, are still commonly seen. Urethane bumper covers do tend to be problematic, however, with cracks and crazing often developing simply from the passage of time. While minor cracks can be repaired, you are usually better off replacing the covers with new ones, which are readily available but somewhat expensive.

Stingray's distinct look came from multiple compound curves that worked together. Only 2,883 1975s were painted Bright Yellow, and with the painted hardtop in place and body-color urethane bumpers, the look is very powerful! For $83, buyers could substitute a vinyl-covered hardtop for the painted one.

1975 Corvette Ratings

Model Comfort/Amenities	****
Reliability	****
Collectibility	**(coupe) ****(convertible)
Parts/Service Availability	****
Est. Annual Maintenance Costs	$400

1975 Corvette Replacement Costs for Common Parts

Convertible top w/pads and straps	$210
Windshield (correct reproduction)	$450
Seat upholstery (pair, correct vinyl)	$250
Seat upholstery (pair, correct leather)	$390
Carpet	$200
Door panels (pair, correct reproduction w/out trim)	$210
Hood	$475
Front fender (correct press-molded reproduction)	$315
Wheel (steel rally wheel)	$125
Headlamp assembly (including cup, ring, adjusters, bezel mount kit, and bulb)	$50
Taillamp lens	$55
Exhaust system (not including catalytic converter)	$275
Shock absorber	$75
Front wheel bearing	$15
Front springs (pair)	$100
Brake master cylinder (functional replacement)	$100
Brake caliper (stainless steel sleeved)	$100
Radiator (Harrison OEM type)	$475
Radiator support	$350
Water pump	$75 (rebuilt original)
Cylinder head (pair)	$200
Rear leaf spring (functional replacement)	$110

Single, large front-fender vents introduced in 1973 were functional. All 1975s displayed the "Stingray" emblem on both fenders. A key switch, which was on the driver side only, controlled the anti-theft alarm system, a feature that was optional beginning in 1968 and has been standard since 1972.

1975 Corvette Specifications

Base price (new)	$6,810.10 (coupe)
	$6,550.10 (convertible)
Production	33,836 (coupe)
	4,629 (convertible)
Engine	V-8
Bore x stroke (inches)	4x3.48
Displacement	350-ci
Compression ratio	8.5:1 (base engine)
Horsepower	165 (base engine)
Transmission	4-speed wide-ratio manual standard, 4-speed close-ratio manual and 3-speed automatic optional
Wheelbase	98 inches
Overall width	69 inches
Overall height	48.1 inches
Overall length	185.2 inches
Track, front	58.7 inches
Track, rear	59.5 inches
Weight	3,690 pounds
Wheels	15x8 inches
Tires	GR70x15 radials
Front suspension	independent unequal length wishbones and coil springs, anti-sway bar, telescopic shock absorbers
Rear suspension	independent radius arms, transverse leaf spring, anti-sway bar half shafts acting as upper locating members, lower transverse rods, telescopic shock absorbers
Steering	recirculating ball
Brakes	4-wheel disc, 4-piston calipers, 11.8-inch rotors front and rear
0 to 60 mph	7.7 seconds (350/165 w/ 2.73:1 axle and automatic transmission)
Standing 1/4-mile	16.1 seconds @ 87.4 mph (350/165 w/ 2.73:1 axle and automatic transmission)
Top speed	129 mph (350/165 w/ 2.73:1 axle and automatic transmission)

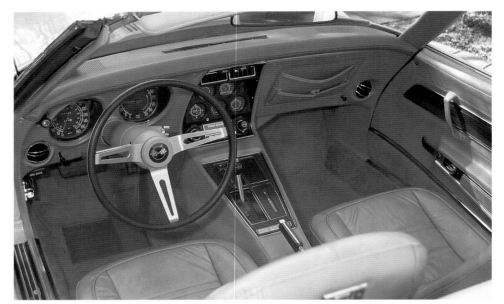

Changes to Corvette's interior for 1975 included the addition of kilometers per hour designations to the speedometer, an "unleaded fuel only" proclamation added to the fuel-gauge face, and a switch to an electronic tachometer that worked in conjunction with HEI ignition.

Unlike earlier C3s, the center console data plate for 1975 did not specify horsepower. This was undoubtedly because the number was embarrassingly low. Besides the actual power reduction—owing mostly to emissions considerations—GM changed the way power was measured. Instead of specifying gross horsepower, which is essentially what the engine generates on a dyno with no accessories installed, they switched to net horsepower, which is what reaches the drive wheels. Net measurement is lower because of power lost to the air cleaner, exhaust system, water pump, alternator, cooling fan, driveline friction, and other components.

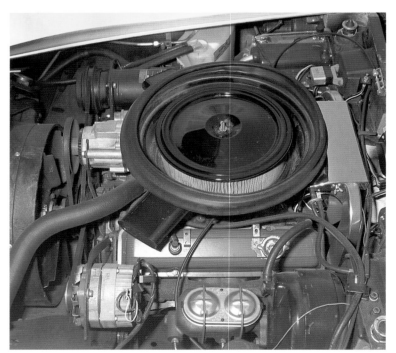

The potent big-block engines offered since 1965 were no longer available in 1975. It was the first time since 1955 that Corvette came with a choice of only two different engines. This L48 has gone less than 4,500 miles since new and is completely original.

1975 Corvette Major Options

Code	Option	Quantity	Price
A31	Power windows	28,745	$93
A85	Deluxe shoulder harness	646	$41
C07	Auxiliary hardtop	2,407	$267
C08	Auxiliary hardtop w/ vinyl trim	279	$350
C50	Rear window defroster	13,760	$46
C60	Air conditioning	31,914	$490
FE7	Gymkhana suspension	3,194	$7
J50	Vacuum power brakes	35,842	$50
L48	350/165-horsepower engine	36,093	standard
L82	350/205-horsepower engine	2,372	$336
M20	Standard 4-speed manual transmission	8,935	no charge
M21	4-speed close-ratio manual transmission (L82 only)	1,057	no charge
M40	Turbo Hydra-Matic transmission	28,473	no charge (L48), $120 (L82)
N37	Tilt & Telescopic steering column	31,830	$82
N41	Power steering	37,591	$129
QRM	GR70-15 white stripe radial tires	5,233	$35
QRN	GR70-15 blackwall radial tires	2,825	no charge
QRZ	GR70-15 white letter radial tires	30,407	$48
U05	Dual horns	22,011	$4
U58	AM-FM stereo radio	24,701	$284
U69	AM-FM radio	12,902	$178
UA1	Heavy-duty battery	16,778	$15
UF1	Map light	21,676	$5
UL5	Radio delete	862	no charge
YF5	California emissions	3,037	$20
Z07	Off-road suspension and brakes*	144	$400
	Rear-axle ratio selection	1,969	$12
	Custom interior w/ leather trim		$154

*Z07 Off-road suspension and brakes was an option package available with L82 only. It included stiffer front and rear springs, heavy-duty shock absorbers, twin-pin front calipers, an extra support for each front caliper, a proportioning valve, and metallic brake pads.

What They Said in 1975

The Corvette feels highly competent, with power-everything to help you guide the long body around as well as an automatic transmission that knows just when you want it to upshift. But its excitement level inevitably sags under the eighth annual repeat of its dated body style. —*Car and Driver,* May 1975

I Bought a 1975 Corvette

I had a 1975 coupe when I was in college, and even though it wasn't really my first choice—it was what I could afford at the time—the car created a lot of good memories. That coupe is long gone, but to bring back the nostalgia of that time with something that's more collectible today, I decided to buy a 1975 convertible. I found it at a vintage Corvette dealer, and though I probably paid a little bit too much, it was too clean and original to resist. Plus, it is yellow, the same color as the coupe I used to have. —Bernard Pasteau

Black, rubber bumper protrusions on both the front and rear urethane bumper covers first appeared in 1975. A one-piece, seamless rear-bumper cover was also new for 1975. The grilles on the rear deck were part of the Astro Ventilation system, which was eliminated after 1975.

More than half the convertibles sold in 1975 came with the optional removable hardtop in addition to a folding soft top. If the original hardtop is missing or if you want to add one to a car that didn't come with it, plan to spend about $2,500 for an excellent example.

Custom Interior Trim included leather seat covers, wood grain appliqués on the door panels and center console, lower carpet trim on door panels, and plusher cut-pile carpeting. It was available in black, silver, medium saddle, dark red, and dark blue.

When evaluating a car for purchase, everyone looks at the convertible top fabric, but few people take the time to properly inspect the remainder of the top assembly. Front and rear bows are prone to rust, weatherstrip is often torn and deteriorated, latches may be broken, and plastic trim is also sometimes broken.

Corvette's heating, ventilation, and air conditioning were manipulated by this somewhat complex control device positioned in front of the shifter. Besides electrical wires, a plethora of vacuum hoses enter and exit the control. Go through all of its settings to learn what is and isn't working.

Corvettes came with either Goodyear Steelgard or Firestone 500 radials in 1975. Original tires like this one are helpful if you show your car at serious venues, but they are not the best choice for a car that is regularly driven. If you buy a car still wearing original tires and will drive it on a regular basis, buy a set of new wheels and tires, thus allowing you to keep the originals intact.

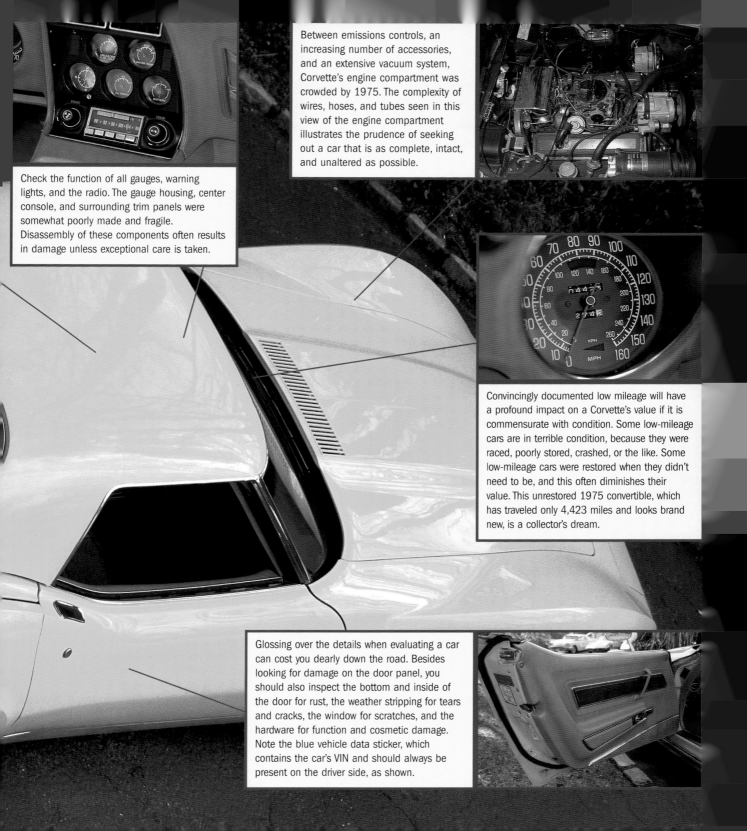

Between emissions controls, an increasing number of accessories, and an extensive vacuum system, Corvette's engine compartment was crowded by 1975. The complexity of wires, hoses, and tubes seen in this view of the engine compartment illustrates the prudence of seeking out a car that is as complete, intact, and unaltered as possible.

Check the function of all gauges, warning lights, and the radio. The gauge housing, center console, and surrounding trim panels were somewhat poorly made and fragile. Disassembly of these components often results in damage unless exceptional care is taken.

Convincingly documented low mileage will have a profound impact on a Corvette's value if it is commensurate with condition. Some low-mileage cars are in terrible condition, because they were raced, poorly stored, crashed, or the like. Some low-mileage cars were restored when they didn't need to be, and this often diminishes their value. This unrestored 1975 convertible, which has traveled only 4,423 miles and looks brand new, is a collector's dream.

Glossing over the details when evaluating a car can cost you dearly down the road. Besides looking for damage on the door panel, you should also inspect the bottom and inside of the door for rust, the weather stripping for tears and cracks, the window for scratches, and the hardware for function and cosmetic damage. Note the blue vehicle data sticker, which contains the car's VIN and should always be present on the driver side, as shown.

Performance was definitely not Corvette's strong point in 1976, but that didn't stop a record number of buyers from flocking to their local Chevrolet dealer that year.

Enthusiasts of open-air motoring look upon 1976 as a very sad year for Corvette—for the first time in the marque's history, a convertible was not produced. Though lamented by collectors in subsequent years, consumers hardly noticed, buying an all-time record number of Corvettes.

While the 1976 model's hood looked the same as the one used from 1973 through 1975, it did not have the cowl induction system the previous ones used. Instead, a plastic duct located above the radiator fed outside air into the carburetor. The system was changed again in 1977, making the hood used in 1976 unique to that year.

Cast aluminum wheels that were supposed to be available beginning in 1973 were finally offered in 1976. Apparently, the quality-control problems that prevented their use earlier had been solved. The wheels were manufactured for Chevrolet by Kelsey-Hayes, the same company that made Corvette's optional knock-off wheels in the 1960s. Cars equipped with the option got only four aluminum rims, with the spare tire still mounted on a steel rim.

The aluminum wheels dramatically changed the car's appearance, making it look much more modern than it did with steel rally wheels, center caps, and trim rings. Besides their cosmetic effect, the aluminum rims also noticeably improved performance by eliminating about 8 pounds of unsprung weight from each wheel assembly.

An unusually high number of 1977-style parts were phased into production toward the end of 1976, so many subtle differences are often seen between early and late 1976 Corvettes. For example, some late 1976s came with the shorter steering column seen in 1977 models. Another example is the interior rearview mirror position. Some late 1976 Corvettes came with the interior rearview mirror mounted directly to the windshield, as is uniformly seen in 1977s, rather than to the upper windshield frame, as was done with earlier 1976 Corvettes.

In keeping with the trend that had been going on since Corvette's very beginning, more and more previously optional equipment and features became standard during 1976.

Power steering, power brakes, and custom leather trim were all listed as optional at the beginning of 1976 but soon became standard. As features became standard, Corvette's list price rose accordingly.

While the 1976 Corvette's interior was essentially the same as in previous models, one important difference caused a lot of controversy. Chevrolet replaced Corvette's traditional hard plastic, three-spoke steering wheel with a padded vinyl, four-spoke design. It wasn't so much the design that incited criticism but rather the fact that the same steering wheel was also used in Chevy's Vega. In response to the outcry, a new, unique-to-Corvette wheel was introduced in 1977.

The biggest challenge for enthusiasts seeking a 1976 today is finding a quality example. Despite the fact that 46,558 were built, not enough high-quality examples survive. Except for special ones like 1975 convertibles and 1978 Indy 500 Pace Car replicas, mid-1970's C3s have historically been the least expensive used Corvettes. This undoubtedly contributed to their scarcity in several ways. The relatively low values tended to encourage people to treat the cars poorly. They were more likely to be owned by young people who were more likely to get into accidents. They were more likely to be used as daily transportation. The low values discouraged people from spending money to properly maintain and restore them, and the low values and accompanying lack of demand dissuaded the restoration parts industry from filling in when Chevrolet discontinued one part after another.

Thankfully, much of this is changing. A 1976 is still worth far less than an otherwise comparable early C3, but values are climbing. Common restoration parts such as seat upholstery, carpet, and weatherstrip are available. Plus, major show organizations including NCRS now recognize 1976s and later C3s.

Additional good news about 1976 Corvettes is that they are still quite affordable and offer an excellent driving experience. Continuing chassis and body improvements, such as the installation of a steel forward-floor section, make them quieter, more rigid, more comfortable, and better handling than earlier Corvettes.

Despite the fact that they are slightly newer and in many ways better built than their predecessors, 1976 Corvettes are still prone to certain problems inherent in the third-generation design. Watch out for rust in the chassis, door frames, windshield frames, radiator support, trailing arms, fuel tank, and front body supports.

Steering boxes tend to wear out with use, and problems are normally evidenced by excessive play, a tight spot, or a notchy feeling when turning. Power steering components and brake calipers frequently leak. Rear-wheel bearings and positraction differentials often need to be rebuilt. Often most frustrating of all, vacuum and electrical system troubles can be difficult to track down and fix.

Emissions-reducing equipment and a large number of features crowded the 1976 engine compartment. This is a completely unrestored and perfectly preserved base L48 engine compartment. The air cleaner was signed for the car's owner by Dave McLellan, chief engineer for Corvette when this 1976 was built.

1976 Corvette Ratings

Model Comfort/Amenities	****
Reliability	****
Collectibility	**
Parts/Service Availability	***
Est. Annual Maintenance Costs	$450

1976 Corvette Replacement Costs for Common Parts

Windshield (correct reproduction)	$450
Seat upholstery (pair, correct vinyl)	$250
Seat upholstery (pair, correct leather)	$390
Carpet	$200
Door panels (pair, correct reproduction w/out trim)	$210
Hood	$475
Front fender (correct press-molded reproduction)	$315
Wheel (steel rally wheel)	$125
Headlamp assembly (including cup, ring, adjusters, bezel mount kit, and bulb)	$50
Taillamp lens	$55
Exhaust system (not including catalytic converter)	$275
Shock absorber	$75
Front wheel bearing	$15
Front springs (pair)	$100
Brake master cylinder (functional replacement)	$100
Brake caliper (stainless steel sleeved)	$100
Radiator (Harrison OEM type)	$475
Radiator support	$350
Water pump	$75 (rebuilt original)
Cylinder head (pair)	$200
Rear leaf spring (functional replacement)	$110

1976 Corvette Specifications

Base price (new)	$7,604.85
Production	46,558
Engine	V-8
Bore x stroke (in inches)	4x3.48
Displacement	350-ci
Compression ratio	8.5:1 (base engine)
Horsepower	180 (base engine)
Transmission	4-speed wide-ratio manual standard, 4-speed close-ratio manual and 3-speed automatic optional
Wheelbase	98 inches
Overall width	69 inches
Overall height	48.1 inches
Overall length	185.2 inches
Track, front	58.7 inches
Track, rear	59.5 inches
Weight	3,655 pounds
Wheels	15x8 inches
Tires	GR70x15 radials
Front suspension	independent unequal length wishbones and coil springs, anti-sway bar, telescopic shock absorbers.
Rear suspension	independent radius arms, transverse leaf spring, anti-sway bar half shafts acting as upper locating members, lower transverse rods, telescopic shock absorbers
Steering	recirculating ball
Brakes	4-wheel disc, 4-piston calipers, 11.8-inch rotors front and rear
0 to 60 mph	7.1 seconds (350/210 w/ 3.36:1 axle and automatic transmission)
Standing 1/4-mile	15.3 seconds @ 91.9 mph (350/210 w/ 3.36:1 axle and automatic transmission)
Top speed	124.5 mph (350/210 w/ 3.36:1 axle and automatic transmission)

The light buckskin leather interior was actually two-tone, because the upper-dash and certain other trim items were a distinctly darker shade of brown compared with the lighter seat covers. A perfect original interior such as this one is highly prized by collectors.

The four-spoke steering wheel used in 1976 models was also used in that year's Chevy Vega, a fact that did not sit well with many Corvette enthusiasts. In 1977, a new wheel was introduced for Tilt & Telescopic steering columns, while standard-column cars still sported the controversial four-spoke wheel.

More than 75 percent of all 1976 Corvettes came with an automatic transmission. Cars equipped with the higher-performance L82 engine had a stronger automatic, which is why Chevrolet charged an extra $134.

A manufacturing-information sticker containing the car's serial number and other information was placed on the driver-side door of every 1976 Corvette. The sticker is usually blue, but variations do exist.

All C3s were well instrumented. With any car you're considering for purchase, closely monitor the gauges, particularly the oil pressure and coolant temperature, while driving and idling.

1976 Corvette Major Options

		Quantity	Price
A31	Power windows	38,700	$107
C49	Rear window defroster	24,960	$78
C60	Air conditioning	40,787	$523
FE7	Gymkhana suspension	5,368	$35
J50	Vacuum power brakes	46,558	$59
L48	350/180-horsepower engine	40,838	standard
L82	350/210-horsepower engine	5,720	$481
M20	Standard 4-speed manual transmission	7,845	no charge
M21	4-speed close-ratio manual transmission (L82 only)	2,088	no charge
M40	Turbo Hydra-Matic transmission	36,625	no charge (base L48, $134 w/ L82)
N37	Tilt & Telescopic steering column	41,797	$95
N41	Power steering	46,385	$151
QRM	GR70-15 white stripe radial tires	3,992	$37
QRN	GR70-15 blackwall radial tires	2,643	no charge
QRZ	GR70-15 white letter radial tires	39,923	$51
U58	AM-FM stereo radio	34,272	$281
U69	AM-FM radio	11,083	$187
UA1	Heavy-duty battery	25,909	$16
UF1	Map light	35,361	$10
UL5	Radio delete	1,203	no charge
YF5	California emissions	3,527	$50
YJ8	Aluminum wheels	6,253	$299
	Rear-axle ratio selection	1,371	$13
	Custom interior w/ leather trim		$164

Most major underhood components installed when the car was new, including the engine block, cylinder heads, intake manifold, exhaust manifolds, radiator, alternator, distributor, water pump, and carburetor, contain a specific part number that is either stamped or cast in. The parts also contain a date code that preceded the final assembly of the car by no more than six months or so.

What They Said in 1976

Expensive, but speed in the same league will cost you half again as much if you buy off the impact rack. —*Car and Driver,* April 1976

I Bought a 1976 Corvette

The Corvette came into our family as a slightly used car in the winter of 1977. I traded in a Volvo wagon and $1,200 to the dealer for it. I loved the car right from the start, but the first time I drove it in the snow, I thought I made a mistake. Snow tires on the back solved that problem, and after that first winter, I just put the car in storage when the first snow came. I also bought a 1996 and, boy, does that car make the 1976 seem old! We still love it, though, and take it out regularly on sunny days. —Robert L. Reddy

A lot of 1976 Corvette buyers are not overly concerned with part numbers and date codes on underhood components, but this is changing as time marches forward. Thus, it is wise to buy a car with as many of its original components intact as find.

A large majority of 1976 Corvettes were equipped with air conditioning, and the system generally worked well when the cars were new. After many years of service, however, it is quite common for the system to stop working. If you're lucky, a simple recharge will fix it. Often, though, comprehensive and expensive work is required.

When this intensive array of tubes, wires, and hoses is all in place and every component is functioning correctly, Corvette engines from the mid-1970s run smoothly and quietly. If you are interested in owning a stock car, you are far better off buying one with all of this in place.

A new air-induction system was used in 1976. It relied on a plastic duct located above the radiator to feed outside air into the carburetor. Because they were used for only one year, some of the components that make up the system are difficult to procure.

All C3s came with very capable four-wheel disc brakes, but old age frequently takes a toll on the system. Check for evidence of leaks beneath the master cylinder and at all four of the calipers. Also look at the hoses and chassis brake lines, which are susceptible to rust.

Body weather stripping is something that many purchasers overlook when inspecting a car. Decades after being manufactured, weather stripping is often dried up and deteriorated. Examine the door, hood, and T-top seals to determine if any need to be replaced.

Vertical scratches in the side windows are a fairly common problem. They are usually caused by contaminants embedded in the window wipe. Minor scratches can be polished out, but deeper ones necessitate replacement of the windows.

When evaluating 1977s, look for the same problems inherent to other C3s. Rust in the chassis, especially in the side rails beneath the rear area of the doors, is a fairly common problem. Rust in the windshield frame, radiator support, front-body support, header bar, and doors is also somewhat common.

From both a mechanical and an exterior styling perspective, the Corvette was relatively unchanged for 1977. Sales increased at a record pace in the years leading up to 1977, so some at GM concluded that it was foolish to meddle with success. In a strange twist, however, even though sales were at an all-time high, they were still quite small by GM's standards. That dissuaded the company from investing the money needed to make substantial changes to a body design entering its tenth year and a chassis going into its fifteenth year.

Even with few changes, 1977s are easily distinguished from other C3s. Instead of being bright silver, the exterior windshield trim was painted satin black. The sunburst-medallion nose emblem introduced in 1973 and used through 1976 was replaced by Corvette's traditional crossed-flag emblem. The "Stingray" script on each front fender was eliminated, and early 1977 Corvettes have no fender emblems at all. Later in the model year, the crossed-flag emblem appeared on both fenders. Also later in the model year, the anti-theft alarm key switch was deleted from the driver-side fender and incorporated into the driver's door lock.

The hood also changed for 1977, with the elimination of the vents at the rear. These served as inlets for the engine's cowl induction system used from 1973 through 1975 but had no purpose after that.

Though the interior's fundamental layout didn't change, quite a few of its parts did. The previously optional custom interior trim was standard, but instead of the faux wood grain appliqués, 1977 got black, satin finished inserts. Seat bottoms and backs were genuine leather, but side panels were again made from vinyl. Cloth-covered seats with leather accents could be substituted for the standard leather seats.

Furthering the effort to update and enhance the interior, Chevy restyled the center console, specified leather for the automatic's shifter boot, added a roof-mounted dome light, and shortened the steering column by about 2 inches to increase interior room and provide for a more arms-extended driving position.

By relocating the parking brake lever slightly and lengthening the four-speed shifter 1 inch, the two were farther apart from one another. The parking brake was thus easier to grasp, and hitting second gear hard no longer resulted in the occasional collision with it.

The interior rearview mirror was mounted on the windshield instead of the windshield frame to reduce its vibration. A new three-spoke, interior-colored, leather-wrapped steering wheel was included with the optional Tilt & Telescopic steering column, but the widely disliked four-spoke wheel shared with Chevy's Vega was still used on the standard column. In addition to being tarnished simply by virtue of its installation in Vegas, the four-spoke wheel did a commendable job of obstructing the driver's view of the instruments.

Proving that Chevy designers were keeping an eye on what automakers abroad were doing, the headlamp and windshield wiper/washer switches were incorporated into a newly designed turn signal lever. Revised sunshades featured a pivoting mount that allowed them to be swung sideways to block annoying sunlight coming in the door windows.

Besides increasing functionality, all of the changes together altered the interior's ambiance. The 1977 interior looks very 1970s and not out of date for the 1980s. By way of contrast, the 1976 interior looked more like 1960s futuristic, which of course is what it was.

An exciting new option, mirrored-glass T-tops, would have updated the exterior countenance to match the interior's new look, but that plan hit a snag. The tops were supposed to be available beginning in 1977, but a dispute over marketing rights between Chevrolet and the supplier led to its cancellation. The vendor did sell them aftermarket, and Chevrolet offered its own glass tops in 1978.

From a collecting perspective, 1977s are in the same category as 1976 Corvettes and 1974 and 1975 coupes. Despite the high production volume, most of these years were driven hard and far, and it is difficult to find a really nice example. Unless you really enjoy the restoration process, you are almost always better off seeking out the highest-quality car you can locate and afford.

Rough specimens needing paint, new interiors, and a lot of mechanical work are quite common, but you need to know what you are in for if you buy one of these intending to properly restore it. You will surely be into the car for a lot more than it is worth if you have to pay a competent shop to do the work. If you do all or most of the labor yourself and enjoy the process, you should not find yourself upside down as far as investment versus value.

The upgraded interior trim that was previously optional became standard fare in 1977. Gone, however, were the faux wood grain appliqués in the door panels and center console, replaced by black inserts. Cloth-covered seats with leather accents could be substituted for the standard leather seats at no extra charge.

1977 Corvette Ratings

Model Comfort/Amenities	****
Reliability	****
Collectibility	***
Parts/Service Availability	****
Est. Annual Maintenance Costs	$450

1977 Corvette Replacement Costs for Common Parts

Windshield (correct reproduction)	$450
Seat upholstery (pair, correct vinyl)	$250
Seat upholstery (pair, correct leather)	$390
Carpet	$200
Door panels (pair, correct reproduction w/out trim)	$210
Hood	$475
Front fender (correct press-molded reproduction)	$315
Wheel (steel rally wheel)	$125
Headlamp assembly (including cup, ring, adjusters, bezel mount kit, and bulb)	$50
Taillamp lens	$55
Exhaust system (not including catalytic converter)	$275
Shock absorber	$75
Front wheel bearing	$15
Front springs (pair)	$100
Brake master cylinder (functional replacement)	$100
Brake caliper (stainless steel sleeved)	$100
Radiator (Harrison OEM type)	$475
Radiator support	$350
Water pump	$75 (rebuilt original)
Ignition shielding	$360
Cylinder head (pair)	$200
Rear leaf spring (functional replacement)	$110
Fuel tank	$200

1977 Corvette Specifications

Base price (new)	$8,647.65
Production	49,213
Engine	V-8
Bore x stroke (small-block, inches)	4x3.48
Displacement (small-block)	350-ci
Compression ratio	8.5:1 (base engine)
Horsepower	180 (base engine)
Transmission	4-speed wide-ratio manual standard, 4-speed close-ratio manual and 3-speed automatic optional
Wheelbase	98 inches
Overall width	69 inches
Overall height	47.7 inches
Overall length	185.2 inches
Track, front	58.7 inches
Track, rear	59.5 inches
Weight	3,550 pounds
Wheels	15x8 inches
Tires	GR70x15 radials
Front suspension	independent unequal length wishbones and coil springs, anti-sway bar, telescopic shock absorbers
Rear suspension	independent radius arms, transverse leaf spring, anti-sway bar half shafts acting as upper locating members, lower transverse rods, telescopic shock absorbers
Steering	recirculating ball
Brakes	4-wheel disc, 4-piston calipers, 11.8-inch rotors front and rear
0 to 60 mph	8.8 seconds (350/210 w/ 3.55:1 axle and automatic transmission)
Standing 1/4-mile	16.6 seconds @ 82.0 mph (350/210 w/ 3.55:1 axle and automatic transmission)
Top speed	122 mph (350/210 w/ 3.55:1 axle and automatic transmission)

The 1977 engine compartment is quite crowded compared with Corvettes from a decade or more earlier. Success at serious shows demands that the car's many underhood components and their finishes are the same as they were when the car was new. This particular engine compartment is one of the finest unrestored examples in existence.

Original paperwork enhances collector interest and increases value. Normally, a build sheet was attached to the gas tank of every car at the factory, so it is somewhat common for this to still be with the car. Other items of paperwork, such as the window sticker, bill of sale, and warranty book are much more difficult to come by.

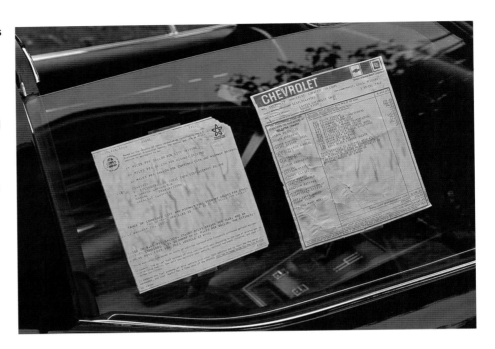

A host of interior revisions improved both the function and appearance of 1977s. The three-spoke steering wheel covered with leather to match the interior color was used only on cars fitted with the optional Tilt & Telescopic steering column, while the widely criticized four-spoke wheel shared with Chevy Vegas was still used with the standard column.

In 1977, Corvettes came with either Goodyear Steelgard or Firestone 500 tires. Original tires are desirable if you intend to show the car at NCRS shows and other serious events. Buy a modern set of radials if you intend to drive the car. Original tires look proper but can pose an increased safety risk.

1977 Corvette Major Options

		Quantity	Price
A31	Power windows	44,341	$116
B32	Floormats	36,763	$22
C49	Electro-Clear rear defogger	30,411	$84
C60	Air conditioning	45,249	$553
D35	Sport mirrors	20,206	$36
FE7	Gymkhana suspension	7,269	$38
G95	Rear-axle ratio selection	972	$14
K30	Cruise-Master speed control	29,161	$88
L48	350/180-horsepower engine	43,065	standard
L82	350/210-horsepower engine	6,148	$495
M20	Standard 4-speed manual transmission	5,922	no charge
M21	4-speed close-ratio manual transmission (L82 only)	2,060	no charge
M40	Turbo Hydra-Matic transmission	41,231	no charge (base L48), $146 (L82)
NA6	High-altitude emissions		$22
N37	Tilt & Telescopic steering column	46,487	$165
QRN	GR70-15 blackwall radial tires	2,986	no charge
QRZ	GR70-15 white letter radial tires	46,227	$57
U58	AM/FM stereo radio	18,483	$281
U69	AM/FM radio	4,700	$187
UM2	AM/FM stereo w/ 8-track	24,603	$414
UA1	Heavy-duty battery	32,882	$17
UL5	Radio delete	1,427	no charge
Y54	Luggage and roof carrier		$73
YF5	California emissions		$70
YJ8	Aluminum wheels	12,646	$321
ZN1	Trailer package	289	$83
ZX2	Convenience package	40,872	$22

What They Said in 1977

Good manners, but not too good manners. . . . Over the years Corvette has matured into a properly buttoned-up boulevardier. —*Car and Driver,* March 1977

I Bought a 1977 Corvette

When I first bought my car from the original owner, it was nothing special to most people. That was in 1988, and it was basically a used car that happened to be in good condition. It only has 42,600 miles on it right now, and I've taken the same kind of care of it that the first owner did. It is a smooth-running and good-handling car that has been very reliable. I changed to stainless steel brakes in 1990, had the air conditioning charged three times, and had a small leak in the radiator repaired. That's all it's needed beyond regular maintenance. —Alton Warwick

If you are buying a car with anything other than documented low mileage, assume you will have to rebuild the differential, steering, suspension, and rear trailing arm assemblies. If the brake calipers have not been stainless steel sleeved, they need to be.

You should always drive a car you're considering for purchase, if possible. Listen for clunking in the rear end, especially when making turns while the rear-end fluid is hot. Feel for slippage in the automatic transmission or clutch while under hard acceleration.

Even though power was relatively low, 1977s were still quick cars by the standards of their day. Four-wheel disc brakes and a competent chassis enable them to stop and handle, too.

As was done previously, seat bottoms and seatbacks were genuine leather, while side panels were made from vinyl. If the seats are in bad condition, plan on replacing the foam as well as the covers. If the car has a problem with rust, you may also need to replace the seat springs.

As with all C3s, the original engine in a 1977 should contain two stampings. One contains the assembly date and application code, while the other contains the car's serial number. In this example, V means the engine was built at the Flint, Michigan, plant; 0507 means it was assembled May 7; and CZK means it's a 350-ci, 180-horsepower engine coupled to a four-speed manual transmission. The latter part of the car's serial number is noted with the 17S437710.

NCRS
Dave MC LELLAN
Mark of Excellence Award

TOP FLIGHT
NCRS

There are several things you should look at in the front of the car with the hood raised. The support structure, header bar, and radiator support are all prone to rust. The headlight assemblies should be evaluated for mechanical function and proper vacuum operation.

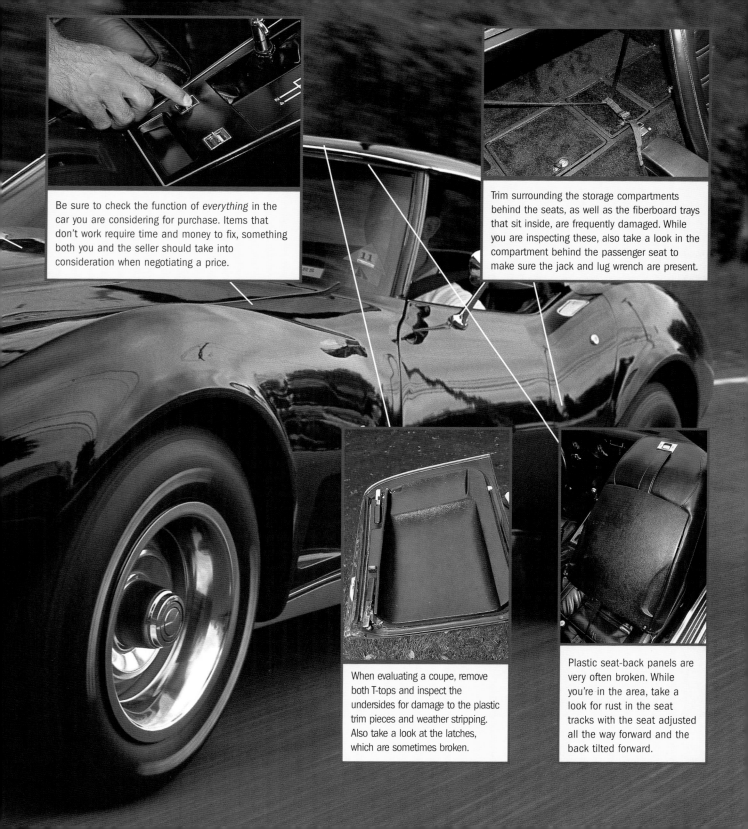

Be sure to check the function of *everything* in the car you are considering for purchase. Items that don't work require time and money to fix, something both you and the seller should take into consideration when negotiating a price.

Trim surrounding the storage compartments behind the seats, as well as the fiberboard trays that sit inside, are frequently damaged. While you are inspecting these, also take a look in the compartment behind the passenger seat to make sure the jack and lug wrench are present.

When evaluating a coupe, remove both T-tops and inspect the undersides for damage to the plastic trim pieces and weather stripping. Also take a look at the latches, which are sometimes broken.

Plastic seat-back panels are very often broken. While you're in the area, take a look for rust in the seat tracks with the seat adjusted all the way forward and the back tilted forward.

The 1978 Indy 500 Pace Car replicas caused a veritable frenzy among speculators and profiteers when they were new, but the hype died down relatively quickly. Though Corvette has paced the Indy 500 four more times since (1986, 1995, 1998, and 2002), 1978 Pace Cars still occupy a special place in the hearts of many collectors.

Corvette's exterior and interior both underwent fairly dramatic changes in 1978. Restyling of the car's rear half incorporated a very large window to create a fastback look that was reminiscent of 1963 through 1967 Corvette coupes. It was a relatively inexpensive way to update a design that was going into its eleventh year of production.

Inside, door panels were completely reconfigured with separate, screwed-on armrests and new integral pulls. Speedometer and tachometer housings were redesigned with a squarer look to match the restyled center console instruments introduced in 1977. In a rather curious turnabout, windshield wiper controls were moved off their steering column stalk and back onto the dash. Also, for the first time since 1967, a real glovebox was added to the passenger side in place of the storage pockets introduced in 1969.

Chevrolet celebrated Corvette's twenty-fifth anniversary in 1978 with a special two-tone Silver Anniversary paint option that featured light silver over dark silver. Almost one-third of the 46,776 1978s produced came with Silver Anniversary paint, so it is by no means rare.

Also in celebration of its twenty-fifth anniversary, Corvette paced the Indy 500 in 1978. As Chevrolet had done with its Camaro in 1969 and as other GM divisions had done with their wares, Chevy offered a limited number of 1978 Indy 500 Pace Car replica Corvettes for sale to the public. After some initial missteps, GM decided to build one replica for each of Chevrolet's 6,000-plus dealers, with the final output reaching 6,502 units.

The most distinguishing feature of the Indy 500 Pace Car replica is its black over silver exterior, a color scheme chosen for no other reason than it appealed to the stylists. A thin red stripe separates the two colors along the body's beltline and complements a red accent stripe around the perimeter of each alloy wheel. The wheels were polished to a beautiful sheen and wore P255 R60x15 Goodyear radials, which were otherwise optional on 1978 Corvettes.

Front and rear body spoilers give the Indy 500 Pace Car replica a purposeful look, and mirrored-glass T-tops make it look more up-to-date than its contemporaries. Adding to the car's rather understated elegance was Chevy's decision to leave the bulk of the special "Indy 500 Pace Car" decals in the packaging for dealer installation if the customer so desired.

The car's special cosmetic treatment carried to the interior, which was molded and stitched together with a rather rich tone of silver that beautifully complemented its exterior. Indy 500 Pace Car replicas sported completely redesigned seats that became standard fare on all Corvettes beginning in 1979. These seats offered much better support and weighed about 12 pounds less than standard 1978 and earlier seats. A commemorative dash plaque attached to the center console read "Limited Edition."

Aside from the unique cosmetic features, all of the Indy 500 Pace Car replicas could be had with or without the various regular production options available on other 1978 Corvettes. These limited edition vehicles, as with all 1978 Corvettes, came standard with an L48 350 engine that delivered 185 horsepower everywhere except in California, where it was rated at 175 horsepower.

Each Indy 500 Pace Car replica received a unique serial number sequence, making it virtually impossible to convincingly convert a regular 1978. Instead of a "4" in the eighth position of the serial number sequence, Indy 500 Pace Car replicas were stamped with a "9."

From a collecting perspective, 1978s have always been popular. Cars optioned with Silver Anniversary paint and, of course, Indy 500 Pace Car replicas are the most popular, especially when fitted with the desirable combination of L82 engine and four-speed transmission.

From a driving perspective, 1978s are a notch above previous C3s in terms of comfort and convenience. The large back window greatly enhanced visibility, and when combined with optional glass T-tops gave Corvette's always-cramped interior a distinctly spacious feel.

Largely because of the twenty-fifth anniversary connection, people tended to treat 1978s more gently than they did previous C3s. As a result, it is a little bit easier to find relatively low-mileage, high-quality examples. As always, you are better off in many ways seeking out and buying an original car that is also in excellent condition.

Though seemingly to a lesser extent than earlier cars, 1978s do still tend to suffer from some inherent problems. Look carefully for rust in the chassis, door frames, radiator support, windshield frame, and trailing arms. Brake calipers inevitably leak from internal corrosion, and the only long-term fix is stainless steel sleeves for the piston bores.

Cast-aluminum valve covers with longitudinal ribs were factory installed on optional L82 engines only. Base L48 engines utilized stamped steel valve covers that were painted GM's corporate engine color. Note all of the different unfinished, painted, and plated surfaces under the hood. This level of detail is necessary if you intend to show your car at serious venues.

1978 Corvette Ratings

Model Comfort/Amenities	****
Reliability	****
Collectibility	*** (Indy 500 Pace Car replicas ****)
Parts/Service Availability	****
Est. Annual Maintenance Costs	$450

1978 Corvette Replacement Costs for Common Parts

Windshield (correct reproduction)	$450
Seat upholstery (pair, correct vinyl)	$250
Seat upholstery (pair, correct leather)	$390
Carpet	$200
Door panels (pair, correct reproduction w/out trim)	$210
Hood	$475
Front fender (correct press-molded reproduction)	$315
Wheel (cast aluminum)	$250
Headlamp assembly (including cup, ring, adjusters, bezel mount kit, and bulb)	$50
Taillamp lens	$55
Exhaust system (not including catalytic converter)	$275
Shock absorber	$75
Front wheel bearing	$15
Front springs (pair)	$100
Brake master cylinder (functional replacement)	$100
Brake caliper (stainless steel sleeved)	$100
Radiator (Harrison OEM type)	$475
Radiator support	$350
Water pump	$75 (rebuilt original)
Cylinder head (pair)	$200
Rear leaf spring (functional replacement)	$110

The 1978 Corvettes handle well, stop superbly, and are reasonably fast, especially when equipped with the optional L82 engine. As a result, a 1978 in proper working order makes for an excellent driver.

Numerous interior features were new for 1978. Highback bucket seats with pronounced bolsters were used in Indy 500 Pace Car replicas only but became standard in all Corvettes beginning in 1979. Mediocre materials often lead to premature wear on many interior surfaces in C3s, and plastic trim items such as the storage compartment door frames are often cracked. For these reasons, pristine interiors such as the one shown are highly desirable.

1978 Corvette Specifications

Base price (new)	$9,351.89
Production	40,274
Engine	V-8
Bore x stroke (small-block, inches)	4x3.48
Displacement (small-block)	350-ci
Compression ratio	8.2:1 (base engine)
Horsepower	185 (base engine)
Transmission	4-speed wide-ratio manual, 4-speed close-ratio manual, or 3-speed automatic
Wheelbase	98 inches
Overall width	69 inches
Overall height	47.9 inches
Overall length	184.7 inches
Track, front	58.7 inches
Track, rear	59.5 inches
Weight	3,585 pounds
Wheels	15x8 inches
Tires	P225/70R15 radials
Front suspension	independent unequal length wishbones and coil springs, anti-sway bar, telescopic shock absorbers
Rear suspension	independent radius arms, transverse leaf spring, anti-sway bar half shafts acting as upper locating members, lower transverse rods, telescopic shock absorbers
Steering	recirculating ball
Brakes	4-wheel disc, 4-piston calipers, 11.8-inch rotors front and rear
0 to 60 mph	7.8 seconds (350/185 w/ 3.08:1 axle and automatic transmission)
Standing 1/4-mile	16.1 seconds @ 88.3 mph (350/185 w/ 3.08:1 axle and automatic transmission)
Top speed	123 mph (350/185 w/ 3.08:1 axle and automatic transmission)

All C3s use the same basic chassis and suspension components, thus they are susceptible to the same problems. The independent rear-suspension setup uses stub axles riding in two bearings on each side. There is no provision to grease these bearings, so they rarely get serviced. You can use a special tool to grease the inner bearing after partial disassembly, but lubricating the outer bearing requires complete disassembly.

Factory ball joints were riveted in place, and replacements are almost always bolted on. Original ball joints in good condition often indicate relatively low mileage, while replaced ball joints often signal high mileage. Because the odometers in C3s can easily be disconnected or turned back, mileage readings are unreliable without additional verification. By examining a myriad of clues, such as the presence or absence of original ball joints, you can reach a logical conclusion regarding the accuracy of the odometer.

Like all C3 Corvettes, 1978s feature highly capable four-wheel disc brakes. Because of an electrolytic reaction between the dissimilar metals used for caliper housings and pistons, corrosion of piston bores is a common problem. The only permanent fix for this is stainless steel sleeved piston bores. If the car you are looking at does not already have stainless steel sleeved calipers, plan on buying them.

1978 Corvette Major Options

Code	Option	Quantity	Price
A31	Power windows	39,931	$130
AU3	Power door locks	12,187	$120
BZ2	25th-anniversary paint	15,283	$399
CC1	Removable glass roof panels	972	$349
C49	Electro-Clear rear defogger	30,912	$95
C60	Air conditioning	37,638	$605
D35	Sport mirrors	38,405	$40
FE7	Gymkhana suspension	12,590	$41
G95	Rear-axle ratio selection	382	$15
K30	Cruise-Master speed control	31,608	$99
L48	350/185-horsepower engine	34,037	standard
L82	350/220-horsepower engine	12,739	$525
M20	Standard 4-speed manual transmission	4,777	no charge
M21	4-speed close-ratio manual transmission (L82 only)	3,385	no charge
M38	Turbo Hydra-Matic transmission	38,614	no charge
NA6	High-altitude emissions		$33
N37	Tilt & Telescopic steering column	37,858	$175
QBS	P255/60R15 white letter radial tires	18,296	$216
QGQ	P225/70R15 blackwall radial tires	2,277	no charge
QGR	P225/70R15 white letter radial tires	26,203	$51
U58	AM-FM stereo radio	10,189	$286
U69	AM-FM radio	2,057	$199
U75	Power antenna	23,069	$49
U81	Dual rear speakers	12,340	$49
UM2	AM-FM stereo w/ 8-track	20,899	$419
UP6	AM-FM stereo w/ CB	7,138	$638
UA1	Heavy-duty battery	28,243	$18
YF5	California emissions		$70
YJ8	Aluminum wheels	28,008	$340
ZN1	Trailer package	972	$89
ZX2	Convenience group	37,222	$84
Z78	Indy 500 Pace Car replica	6,502	$13,653.21

What They Said in 1978

It would take somebody with a pretty exquisite viewpoint and surfeit of chutzpah to call the whole thing a bum idea now. Imagine being such a thundering success that you can make a big deal out of some extra rear glass, a glovebox, and an enlarged tailpipe! Yet there she stands, groomed and ready for the faithful with $11,388 worth of standard equipment and options—and GM will sell just about every one of the 43,000 or so it produces this year. —*Road & Track*, April 1978

I Bought a 1978 Corvette

I bought my Pace Car new, and my only regret is not getting a four-speed. At the time, I thought I would drive the car pretty regularly and thought the automatic would be more convenient. I got every available option, including the stereo with CB radio and cruise control. I did not put the stickers on and am glad that I didn't. We have enjoyed driving the car and now get a kick out of bringing it to local shows a few times each year. It's funny how the car still feels new to me after all these years, yet it really is a classic now. —Frank Crum

All 1978 through 1982 Corvettes are equipped with a space-saver Goodyear Polyspare spare tire sized at P195/80D15. Regardless of what type of wheels the car is fitted with, the space-saver spare is mounted to a semi-black 15X5-inch stamped steel rim. Some very early 1978 Corvettes have a spare-tire rim that is painted bright yellow instead of black.

Test the function of all components and systems when inspecting a car for purchase. Power windows were still optional in 1978, as was AM/FM stereo with integral CB radio. Both are prone to failure after more than 25 years of service and are usually expensive to fix.

OFFICIAL PACE CAR
62nd ANNUAL INDIANAPOLIS 500 MILE RACE

Fiberglass doesn't rust, but the steel used throughout 1978 Corvettes may. T-top seals deteriorate and allow water into the cockpit. The water accumulates on the floor, which results in rust in the seat tracks.

All C3 Corvettes rely on an unusual parking brake system. The insides of the rear rotors are machined to act like small drums. Equally small shoes and accompanying hardware are housed inside the drums. When you pull the parking brake handle, you move a cable that activates the shoes. Severe rust is a common problem with the shoe hardware, and while replacement parts made from stainless steel are available, installing them is labor intensive.

This horn button is painted to match interior color, and features an emblem commemorating Corvette's 25th anniversary in 1978. All 1978 Corvettes came with dual horns mounted behind the front grille area, and you should make sure they work. Over time, internal rust can render the horns silent. Problems are also sometimes found in the horn button, horn relay, or wiring.

Rubber bushings are used extensively throughout Corvette's chassis, and they're likely to fail over time. New bushings are inexpensive, but the labor to install them usually isn't. Unless they have already been replaced, any C3 you look at will need at least some new bushings.

Shims located between the upper control arm mount and chassis adjust the front wheel alignment. More than four or five shims at any one location, or a large disparity in the number of shims at different locations, often indicates a serious problem with the front end or chassis.

While lacking the raw power of early C3s, 1979s still offer decent acceleration and top out north of 120 miles per hour. Equally important, they handle and brake extremely well and provide a very good ride.

Over its 50-plus year history, Corvette has had a number of "in-between" years that enthusiasts have regularly bypassed, and 1979 is one of those semi-forgotten years. Nonetheless, there were a number of changes that make 1979s interesting and worthwhile acquisitions.

Front and rear spoilers included on 1978 Indy Pace Car replicas became an option that could be added to any 1979. Besides giving the cars a more purposeful countenance, the spoilers also gave a functional benefit. Together, they yielded a drop in the car's coefficient of drag by about 15 percent and resulted in a fuel economy gain of about one-half mile per gallon.

The special seats utilized in the 1978 Indy 500 Pace Car replicas, featuring pronounced side bolsters and highbacks that folded in the middle to allow easy access to the rear storage area, became standard fare in 1979. Besides offering greater support, they were about 12 pounds lighter than the seats they replaced. Weight savings came largely from extensive use of plastic and elimination of the seatback locking mechanism, which was replaced by an inertia-type lock system.

The reduction in weight afforded by the new seats was important not only for performance but also because, like every other car maker, GM was affected by the government's corporate-average fuel economy regulations that went into effect beginning in 1978. Weight lost translated into miles per gallon gained.

Continuing the long-established trend toward more features and greater luxury, an AM-FM radio finally became standard in 1979. Tungsten-halogen high-beam headlamps, which gave noticeably better visibility at night, were used beginning midyear. An illuminated mirror for the passenger-side sun visor was offered as an option for the first time.

The base L48 350-ci engine was rated at 195 horsepower, 10 more than previously. Once again, the 350-ci L82 engine was optional, and at 225 horsepower, it produced 5 more horsepower than in 1978. The modest power gain in the L82 was attributed to a more efficient muffler design.

The base engine also benefited from the less-restrictive mufflers as well as installation of the same low-restriction, dual-air intake previously used only with the L82.

As in the past, neither a four-speed manual transmission nor an L82 engine could be ordered for cars sold in California or in high-altitude (4,000 feet above sea level) locales because of federal and state emissions regulations. The close-ratio four-speed was offered at no additional cost but could only be coupled with the L82.

Because the hideaway headlamps, HVAC controls, and much of the extensive anti-pollution equipment found on them are vacuum controlled, 1979 Corvettes are prone to vacuum leaks and other vacuum system problems. Using a gauge to measure manifold vacuum will usually reveal malfunctions in the system and can tell you something about the engine's internal condition.

As always, carefully inspect the body of any prospective purchase to determine if it has been involved in a serious collision. Besides looking for telltale signs of poor body repair, which is sometimes evident through the paint, it is advisable to inspect as much of the underside of the body as you can. With the car up on a lift or you down on your back, use a portable light to look up in the wheel housings as well as underneath the nose and rear sections of the body. The underside of all panels should be dark gray in color, relatively smooth, and free of any sort of repairs.

While you are probing from beneath, also take a look at the chassis for signs of rust, especially in the side rails beneath and toward the rear of the doors. In addition, look for rust on the bottom of the fuel tank, in the radiator support, and in the trailing arms. Also while underneath, examine the engine, transmission, differential, air conditioning/heater exchange box, power steering, radiator, fuel tank, and master cylinder for any signs of fluid leakage.

Corvettes for 1979 may not have the collector appeal of an early big-block, a 1975 convertible, a 1978 Indy 500 Pace Car replica, or a 1982 Collector Edition, but neither does it have the relatively high price tag of these other cars.

It's the kind of Corvette you can take anywhere and leave parked anywhere without a worry or a care. It's the kind of car that can be used exactly the way Corvettes were meant to be used in the first place.

The highback bucket seats first seen in 1978 Indy 500 Pace Car replicas offered greater support than previous seats. Seat backs that pivoted at the halfway point allowed for improved access to the storage area in the rear of the body. Outer side bolsters often wear first from people scraping across them when entering and exiting the car.

1979 Corvette Ratings

Model Comfort/Amenities	****
Reliability	****
Collectibility	***
Parts/Service Availability	****
Est. Annual Maintenance Costs	$450

1979 Corvette Replacement Costs for Common Parts

Windshield (correct reproduction)	$450
Seat upholstery (pair, correct vinyl)	$250
Seat upholstery (pair, correct leather)	$390
Carpet	$200
Door panels (pair, correct reproduction w/out trim)	$210
Hood	$475
Front fender (correct press-molded reproduction)	$315
Wheel (cast aluminum)	$250
Headlamp assembly (including cup, ring, adjusters, bezel mount kit, and bulb)	$50
Taillamp lens	$55
Exhaust system (not including catalytic converter)	$275
Shock absorber	$75
Front wheel bearing	$15
Front springs (pair)	$100
Brake master cylinder (functional replacement)	$100
Brake caliper (stainless steel sleeved)	$100
Radiator (Harrison OEM type)	$475
Radiator support	$350
Water pump	$75 (rebuilt original)
Cylinder head (pair)	$200
Rear leaf spring (functional replacement)	$110

1979 Corvette Specifications

Base price (new)	$10,220.23
Production	53,807
Engine	V-8
Bore x stroke (inches)	4x3.48
Displacement	350-ci
Compression ratio	8.25:1 (base engine)
Horsepower	195 (base engine)
Transmission	4-speed wide-ratio manual, 4-speed close-ratio manual, or 3-speed automatic
Wheelbase	98 inches
Overall width	69 inches
Overall height	47.7 inches
Overall length	184.7 inches
Track, front	58.7 inches
Track, rear	59.5 inches
Weight	3,745 pounds
Wheels	15x8 inches
Tires	P225/70R15 radials
Front suspension	independent unequal-length wishbones and coil springs, anti-sway bar, telescopic shock absorbers
Rear suspension	independent radius arms, transverse leaf spring, anti-sway bar half shafts acting as upper locating members, lower transverse rods, telescopic shock absorbers
Steering	recirculating ball
Brakes	four-wheel disc, 4-piston calipers, 11.8-inch rotors front and rear
0 to 60 mph	6.6 seconds (350/225 w/ 3.55:1 axle and automatic transmission)
Standing 1/4-mile	15.6 seconds @ 91.0 mph (350/225 w/ 3.55:1 axle and automatic transmission)
Top speed	121 mph (350/225 w/ 3.55:1 axle and automatic transmission)

With plastic ignition shielding and blue valve covers, the base L48 engine didn't look like much. Gone were the days when even the standard engine was all dressed up with chrome and decals declaring horsepower.

A red leather interior looks especially rich against silver exterior. As with all C3 Corvettes, interiors tend to look shabby ahead of schedule. Seat covers, carpeting, and all soft-trim items are readily available, but costs add up pretty quickly. For this reason, you are always better off paying more up front for a car that needs little or nothing.

Chevrolet's small-block V-8, introduced in 1955, is among the most successful powerplants in automotive history. Engines that are reasonably well-maintained will give many years and many miles of faithful service.

Front and rear spoilers that first appeared on 1978 Indy 500 Pace Car replicas were optional on all 1979s, but the vast majority of buyers did not order them. Perhaps they preferred the clean look of the body without the spoilers.

Evaluation of any prospective purchase should include inspection of all fluids, including brake fluid, transmission fluid, engine oil, and engine coolant. If you discover significantly dirty brake fluid in the master cylinder, plan on performing a thorough brake service.

1979 Corvette Major Options

		Quantity	Price
A31	Power windows	20,631	$141
AU3	Power door locks	9,054	$131
CC1	Removable glass roof panels	14,480	$365
C49	Electro-Clear rear defogger	41,587	$102
C60	Air conditioning	47,136	$635
D35	Sport mirrors	48,211	$45
D80	Front and rear spoilers	6,853	$265
F51	Heavy-duty shock absorbers	2,164	$33
FE7	Gymkhana suspension	12,321	$49
G95	Rear-axle ratio selection	428	$19
K30	Cruise-Master speed control	34,445	$113
L48	350/195-horsepower engine	39,291	standard
L82	350/225-horsepower engine	14,516	$565
M20	Standard 4-speed manual transmission	8,291	no charge
M21	4-speed close-ratio manual transmission (L82 only)	4,062	no charge
M38	Turbo Hydra-Matic transmission	41,454	no charge
NA6	High-altitude emissions		$35
N37	Tilt & Telescopic steering column	47,463	$190
N90	Aluminum wheels	33,741	$380
QBS	P255/60R15 white letter radial tires	17,920	$226.20
QGQ	P225/70R15 blackwall radial tires	6,284	no charge
QGR	P225/70R15 white letter radial tires	29,603	$55
U58	AM-FM stereo radio	9,256	$90
U69	AM-FM radio	6,523	$199
U75	Power antenna	35,730	$52
U81	Dual rear speakers	37,754	$52
UM2	AM-FM stereo w/ 8-track	21,435	$228
UN3	AM-FM stereo w/ cassette	12,110	$234
UP6	AM-FM Stereo w/ CB	4,483	$439
UA1	Heavy-duty battery	3,405	$21
YF5	California emissions		$83
ZN1	Trailer package	1,001	$98
ZQ2	Power windows and door locks	28,465	$272
ZX2	Convenience group	41,530	$94

What They Said in 1979

A time proven engine with a sturdy transmission, reasonably good suspension enhanced by tires with a very large footprint—these are the things that made us optimistic about the Corvette. But after three days and more than 1,000 miles, we could say only that the gearbox, heating and ventilation systems are first rate. —*Road & Track*, April 1979

I Bought a 1979 Corvette

I was looking for a later shark-style project car when I found a 1979 in the paper. It needed almost everything redone, and it took me about two years of working on it in my free time to get it just about finished. The only thing I would do differently if I bought another one is I would get one that had nice paint on it. I did a lot of the stripping and preparation work myself, and that was the only part of the project I didn't enjoy. Plus, even though I did a lot of work, it was still expensive to get it painted. —Steven Kiser

1979 Garage Watch

Run the engine and monitor the gauges to make sure they work and to evaluate engine oil pressure, cooling system effectiveness, and charging system function. Also try the radio and go through all of the HVAC functions. Because of Corvette's confined packaging, even small problems in the HVAC can require a huge amount of time to remedy.

Remove both T-tops and examine their undersides for any damage to hardware or weather-stripping seals. Problems with the seals allow water in, and that leads to further problems, including ruined upholstery and carpeting, rust in the seat frames, and rust in the roof's steel structure.

C3 Corvettes that were stored in destructive environments or regularly driven on salted roads are likely to have at least some rust in the chassis and its components. Surface rust is not going to affect the function or safety of the car, but more severe corrosion can be a never-ending problem. The boxed-in section holding the rear-spring mount bolt is the back of the trailing arm, a component that is susceptible to rust. The layers of rust building between the folded-over segments of the trailing arm are cause for concern and warrant closer inspection of the entire underside.

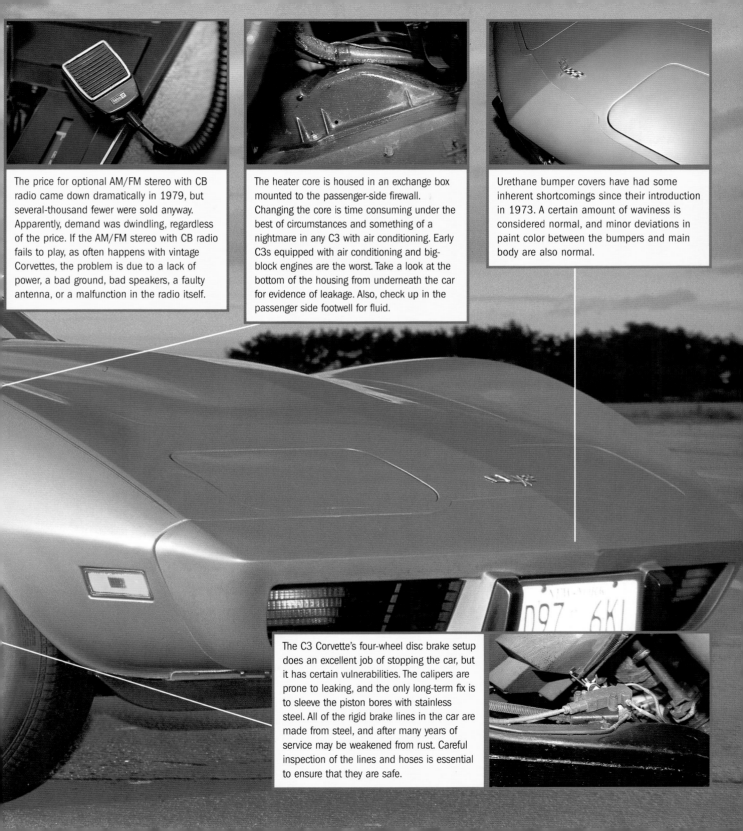

The price for optional AM/FM stereo with CB radio came down dramatically in 1979, but several-thousand fewer were sold anyway. Apparently, demand was dwindling, regardless of the price. If the AM/FM stereo with CB radio fails to play, as often happens with vintage Corvettes, the problem is due to a lack of power, a bad ground, bad speakers, a faulty antenna, or a malfunction in the radio itself.

The heater core is housed in an exchange box mounted to the passenger-side firewall. Changing the core is time consuming under the best of circumstances and something of a nightmare in any C3 with air conditioning. Early C3s equipped with air conditioning and big-block engines are the worst. Take a look at the bottom of the housing from underneath the car for evidence of leakage. Also, check up in the passenger side footwell for fluid.

Urethane bumper covers have had some inherent shortcomings since their introduction in 1973. A certain amount of waviness is considered normal, and minor deviations in paint color between the bumpers and main body are also normal.

The C3 Corvette's four-wheel disc brake setup does an excellent job of stopping the car, but it has certain vulnerabilities. The calipers are prone to leaking, and the only long-term fix is to sleeve the piston bores with stainless steel. All of the rigid brake lines in the car are made from steel, and after many years of service may be weakened from rust. Careful inspection of the lines and hoses is essential to ensure that they are safe.

Corvette's body underwent a serious facelift in 1980 with the incorporation of integral spoilers front and rear. The new look was sleeker and more aggressive.

Corvette underwent a number of significant changes in 1980. Most, but not all, of these were tied in with the never-ending battle to comply with stricter fuel economy and emissions standards.

The previously optional add-on front and rear spoilers first seen on the 1978 Indy Pace Car replicas and offered as optional in 1979 were made integral with the surrounding bodywork. Combined with a revised front grille, the new body design yielded a drop in the car's coefficient of drag from 0.503 to a still not great but nonetheless better 0.443. The lower drag resulted in a fuel economy gain of about 5 percent, and the molded-in-front spoiler also gave the added benefit of 50 percent more airflow to the radiator.

Finally, besides all of the functional advantages, the new look created by the integral spoilers was also widely acclaimed from a cosmetic perspective. It was at the same time both more refined and more aggressive.

Interior changes for 1980 included joining of the middle and passenger-side storage bins located behind the seats into a single compartment, relocation of the power door-lock button, and revision of the speedometer face to only read to 85 miles per hour. The speedometer change was actually phased in beginning late in 1979.

Air conditioning, offered as an option since 1963, was finally made standard in 1980. The previously optional Tilt & Telescopic steering column, power windows, sport mirrors, and ZX2 Convenience Group items were also installed in every 1980 as standard equipment. All of these features, as well as the incorporation of the spoilers into the new bodywork, account for much of Corvette's hefty $2,920 price increase from 1979 to 1980.

The increasing number of standard features made it all the more difficult for engineers to reduce the car's weight. Nonetheless, eliminating mass was essential if Corvette was to maintain its performance and meet ever-stricter fuel economy and emissions requirements. In testimony to their efforts, a total of about 250 pounds were shed in 1980.

Most of the weight savings came from extensive use of aluminum in spots where steel or iron had been used previously. For example, the differential housing and cross member were both made from aluminum, and the base L48 engine's cast-iron intake manifold was replaced by the optional L82 engine's aluminum intake.

Additional weight savings came from the use of lower-density material for Corvette's removable roof panels, which had the added benefit of making removal and installation of the panels easier. Thinner hoods and outer door panels also contributed to a lower overall weight in 1980.

In a rather sad reflection of just how far ahead of available technology California's emissions requirements were at the time, all 1980 Corvettes sold new in that state had to have a special 305-ci engine in place of the normal 350. The California engine utilized stainless steel tubular headers and represented the first use of an oxygen sensor in a closed-loop system.

The California-mandated 305 could only be coupled to an automatic transmission and was rated at 180 horsepower. Interestingly, this was only 10 horsepower less than the 49-state L48 350 engine. Did the 12.86 percent reduction in displacement and additional emissions equipment really result in a loss of only 10 horsepower, or did Chevrolet manipulate the numbers in order to least offend performance-minded buyers in California?

In keeping with the general trend, Corvette's overall quality improved in 1980. For example, for the first time, body panels used for the nose and roof were manufactured using urethane. This modification to the molding process yielded smoother paint surfaces with fewer imperfections.

Though all of the problems inherent to earlier C3s were still present through the end of the model's life in 1982, their occurrence in most cases diminished markedly during the final years. This was a result of steadily improving quality and also the simple fact that later cars are that much newer than earlier ones, and therefore have that many fewer years of use and abuse.

Potential problems to look for when considering a car

for purchase include rust in the chassis, windshield frame radiator support, and trailing arms. The highback seats first seen in 1978 Indy Pace Car replicas are prone to excessive wear on the outer bolsters from people rubbing against them as they enter and exit the car. Collision damage to the body and frame is always a concern, and careful inspection by a knowledgeable observer will almost always reveal the presence of a problem in this area.

The 1980 Corvette interior was little changed from that used in 1979. Previously optional power windows, air conditioning, and Tilt & Telescopic steering column were all made standard this year.

1980 Corvette Ratings

Model Comfort/Amenities	★★★★★
Reliability	★★★★
Collectibility	★★★
Parts/Service Availability	★★★★
Est. Annual Maintenance Costs	$450

1980 Corvette Replacement Costs for Common Parts

Windshield (correct reproduction)	$450
Seat upholstery (pair, correct vinyl)	$250
Seat upholstery (pair, correct leather)	$390
Carpet	$200
Door panels (pair, correct reproduction w/out trim)	$210
Hood	$475
Front fender (correct press-molded reproduction)	$315
Wheel (cast aluminum)	$250
Headlamp assembly (including cup, ring, adjusters, bezel mount kit, and bulb)	$50
Taillamp lens	$55
Exhaust system (not including catalytic converter)	$275
Shock absorber	$75
Front wheel bearing	$15
Front springs (pair)	$100
Brake master cylinder (functional replacement)	$100
Brake caliper (stainless steel sleeved)	$100
Radiator (Harrison OEM type)	$475
Radiator support	$350
Water pump	$75 (rebuilt original)
Cylinder head (pair)	$200
Rear leaf spring (functional replacement)	$110

1980 Corvette Specifications

Base price (new)	$13,140.24
Production	40,614
Engine	V-8
Bore x stroke (in inches)	4x3.48
Displacement	350-ci
Compression ratio	8.5:1 (base engine)
Horsepower	190 (base engine)
Transmission	4-speed manual or automatic standard
Wheelbase	98 inches
Overall width	69 inches
Overall height	48.1 inches
Overall length	185.3 inches
Track, front	58.7 inches
Track, rear	59.5 inches
Weight	3,330 pounds
Wheels	15x8 inches
Tires	P225/70R15 radials
Front suspension	independent unequal length wishbones and coil springs, anti-sway bar, telescopic shock absorbers
Rear suspension	independent radius arms, transverse leaf spring, anti-sway bar half shafts acting as upper locating members, lower transverse rods, telescopic shock absorbers
Steering	recirculating ball
Brakes	four-wheel disc, 4-piston calipers, 11.8-inch rotors front and rear
0 to 60 mph	7.6 seconds (350/190 w/ 3.07:1 axle and 4-speed manual transmission)
Standing 1/4[fraction font]-mile	15.9 seconds @ 88.0 mph (350/190 w/ 3.07:1 axle and 4-speed manual transmission)
Top speed	123 mph (350/190 w/ 3.07:1 axle and 4-speed manual transmission)

Because so much equipment was included as standard fare and because of all the emissions-reducing apparatus, Corvette's engine compartment seemed to get more crowded every year. The aluminum intake manifold previously used only with the optional high-performance L82 was now used for the base engine as well. This was part of Chevrolet's effort to trim weight from Corvette.

Aluminum wheels were still an option in 1980. Raised white-letter Goodyear Polysteel Radials were also an extra-cost option. Original tires are highly desirable to collectors but should not be driven on with any regularity. In the interests of both safety and preserving the tires, a second set of wheels fitted with new radials is recommended.

A new rear fascia in concert with new front-body treatment yielded a 12 percent improvement in coefficient of drag. The new front also afforded 50 percent better airflow to the radiator. Waves in the urethane bumper covers, seen here, are considered normal.

Original mufflers bearing the manufacturing date January 1980 testify to this car's extremely low mileage and meticulous care. Always make sure that the spare tire is present when inspecting a car. All 1978 through 1982 Corvettes came with a Goodyear Polyspare space-saver spare tire mounted on a black rim.

Because of strict emissions standards there, Chevrolet did not certify its 350-ci engine for sale in California. Instead, all Corvettes sold new in California were equipped with 305-ci engines. If California buyers wanted the optional L82, they had to move to another state or find a way to wiggle around the law.

1980 Corvette Major Options

		Quantity	Price
AU3	Power door locks	32,692	$140
CC1	Removable glass roof panels	19,695	$391
C49	Electro-Clear rear defogger	36,589	$109
F51	Heavy-duty shock absorbers	1,695	$35
FE7	Gymkhana suspension	9,907	$55
K30	Cruise-Master speed control	30,821	$123
LG4	305/180-horsepower engine	3,221	–$50
L82	350/225-horsepower engine	5,069	$595
M18	4-speed manual transmission	5,726	no charge
M33	Turbo Hydra-Matic transmission (California)		no charge
MV4	Turbo Hydra-Matic transmission	34,838	no charge
N90	Aluminum wheels	34,128	$407
QGQ	P225/70R15 blackwall radial tires	1,266	no charge
QGR	P225/70R15 white letter radial tires	26,208	$62
QXH	P255/60R15 white letter radial tires	13,140	$426.16
U58	AM-FM stereo radio	6,138	$46
U69	AM-FM radio	985	no charge
U75	Power antenna	32,863	$56
U81	Dual rear speakers	36,650	$52
UA1	Heavy-duty battery	1,337	$22
UL5	Radio delete (credit)	201	–$126
UM2	AM-FM stereo w/ 8-track	15,708	$155
UN3	AM-FM stereo w/ cassette	15,148	$168
UP6	AM-FM stereo w/ CB	2,434	$391
V54	Roof panel carrier	3,755	$125
YF5	California emissions	3,221	$250
ZN1	Trailer package	796	$105

What They Said in 1980

America's only sports car, but that doesn't excuse everything.
—*Car and Driver*, May 1980

I Bought a 1980 Corvette

I originally brought my car to autocross on weekends, and after two seasons, I restored it for street use only. The best parts of the car from a performance standpoint are the handling and braking. Acceleration is decent and can be improved on a lot if you're willing to deviate from the stock parts. Maintenance is actually pretty simple and inexpensive if you take care of small problems before they get to be big problems. After a lot of street miles, two full seasons of autocrossing, and then a lot more miles, the car has a few creaks and groans but overall has held up very well. —Lisa Crevecchio

Even though the fit and finish of body panels were better than what came before, 1980 Corvettes were still not particularly good. This is how the corner of the hood mates to the fender on an original-paint, completely undamaged 1980 with 7,500 miles.

1980 Garage Watch

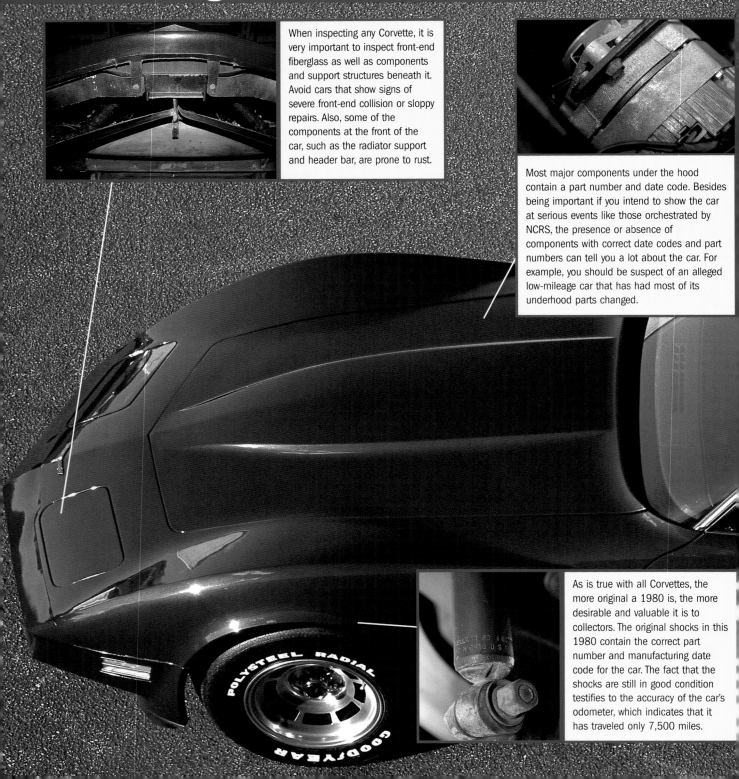

When inspecting any Corvette, it is very important to inspect front-end fiberglass as well as components and support structures beneath it. Avoid cars that show signs of severe front-end collision or sloppy repairs. Also, some of the components at the front of the car, such as the radiator support and header bar, are prone to rust.

Most major components under the hood contain a part number and date code. Besides being important if you intend to show the car at serious events like those orchestrated by NCRS, the presence or absence of components with correct date codes and part numbers can tell you a lot about the car. For example, you should be suspect of an alleged low-mileage car that has had most of its underhood parts changed.

As is true with all Corvettes, the more original a 1980 is, the more desirable and valuable it is to collectors. The original shocks in this 1980 contain the correct part number and manufacturing date code for the car. The fact that the shocks are still in good condition testifies to the accuracy of the car's odometer, which indicates that it has traveled only 7,500 miles.

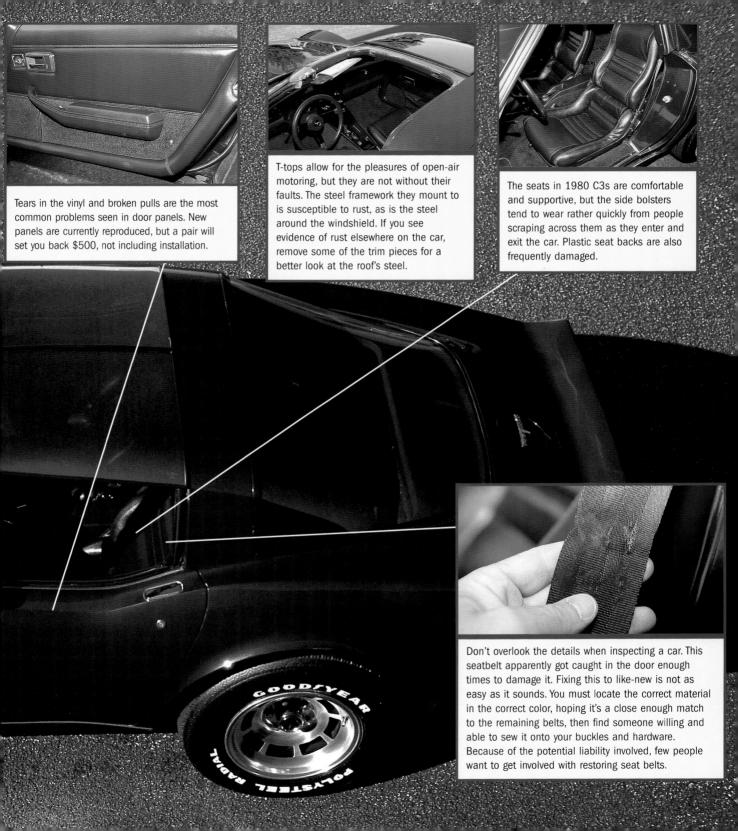

Tears in the vinyl and broken pulls are the most common problems seen in door panels. New panels are currently reproduced, but a pair will set you back $500, not including installation.

T-tops allow for the pleasures of open-air motoring, but they are not without their faults. The steel framework they mount to is susceptible to rust, as is the steel around the windshield. If you see evidence of rust elsewhere on the car, remove some of the trim pieces for a better look at the roof's steel.

The seats in 1980 C3s are comfortable and supportive, but the side bolsters tend to wear rather quickly from people scraping across them as they enter and exit the car. Plastic seat backs are also frequently damaged.

Don't overlook the details when inspecting a car. This seatbelt apparently got caught in the door enough times to damage it. Fixing this to like-new is not as easy as it sounds. You must locate the correct material in the correct color, hoping it's a close enough match to the remaining belts, then find someone willing and able to sew it onto your buckles and hardware. Because of the potential liability involved, few people want to get involved with restoring seat belts.

In 1981, Corvette production transitioned from St. Louis, Missouri, where it had been since 1954, to a new factory in Bowling Green, Kentucky. Two-tone paint combinations, which were offered as optional beginning in 1981, were only supposed to have been on Bowling Green cars, but rumors of factory two-tones coming out of St. Louis persist.

During the 1981 model year, Corvette assembly transitioned from St. Louis, Missouri, where it had been since 1954, to a new home in Bowling Green, Kentucky. All St. Louis-built Corvettes were painted in acrylic lacquer, while all Bowling Green cars were done in urethane enamel base coats topped by urethane enamel clear coat. According to published data, optional two-tone color combinations were available only on Bowling Green cars, but a number of St. Louis two-tones are believed to have also been built.

For the first time since 1955, no optional powerplants were offered in a Corvette. Each car was equipped with a 350-ci engine rated at 190 horsepower. This was the final year Corvette engines relied on a carburetor for fuel delivery. Even though the carburetor was electronically governed, to some extent it was still a carburetor and not true fuel injection.

This was the final year a manual transmission was offered until after the start of 1984 production. Fuel economy and emissions issues were the primary factors that led to the four-speed manual's temporary disappearance following 1981.

All 1981 engines came with the same type of stainless steel headers utilized on 305 engines that went to California in 1980. The primary advantage of these headers was their reduced mass when compared with more traditional cast-iron exhaust manifolds.

Corvette's weight-loss regimen continued in 1981 with other innovations besides the tubular headers. Previously used cast aluminum and stamped steel valve covers were replaced with cast magnesium covers. Thinner glass for doors and roof panels, which was phased in late in 1980, was used on all 1981s. Cars equipped with standard suspension and automatic transmission got a fiberglass-reinforced monoleaf rear spring in place of the heavy steel spring. The new spring weighed only 8 pounds versus the steel unit's 44 pounds.

The weight savings benefited performance, but the most compelling motivation was Chevrolet's need to control its corporate-average fuel economy and meet ever-tightening emissions regulations.

Another factor that ultimately helped performance while improving fuel mileage and reduced tailpipe emissions was electronic engine and drivetrain management. All 1980 Corvettes sold new in California were fitted with GM's new Computer Command Control system. For 1981, this system was standard on all Corvettes as well as other GM vehicles. It adjusted ignition timing and provided more-precise fuel metering in order to govern the air/fuel ratio. It also regulated lockup of the automatic transmission's torque-converter clutches, which were themselves a new innovation introduced in 1981. Though incredibly crude by today's standards—it could make only 10 adjustments per second—the Computer Command Control's functions did improve economy while reducing emissions.

Corvette's interior underwent some noteworthy changes in 1981. A power, adjustable driver seat was offered for the first time, and nearly three-quarters of buyers thought it was worth the extra money. A quartz clock was standard, and all optional radios except the U58 AM-FM stereo utilized Delco's electronic-tuned receivers. These new electronic-tuned radios had an integral clock, so Corvettes equipped with them did not have the standard quartz instrument panel clock. An engine oil temperature gauge was installed where the standard clock otherwise went.

Other changes to 1981's interior consisted of color keying the headlight and windshield wiper switch bezels to the interior color. In the past, these bezels were black, regardless of interior color.

As with most C3s made after 1972, 1981s are not especially desirable to collectors at the present. There are, however, definite indications that collector interest is slowly but steadily rising. Predictably, the most desirable examples are wonderfully preserved, highly optioned, low-mileage originals painted and trimmed in appealing colors.

The flip side of relatively little hardcore collector interest is that 1981s remain quite affordable. In addition, like all later C3s, the 1981s have enough creature comforts and enough of a modern feel to make them very competent, enjoyable drivers.

When considering a car for purchase, look carefully at areas known to be problematic on C3s. Be aware of chassis rust in the side rails beneath the rear portion of the doors, as well as rust in the door housings, windshield frame, radiator support, and tailing arms. Brake caliper leakage from piston bore corrosion is common, so if the car does not already have stainless steel sleeved brakes, it will need them. And, of course, don't forget to run and drive the car at full operating temperature to evaluate the function of all mechanical and electrical systems.

1981 Corvette Ratings

Model Comfort/Amenities	*****
Reliability	****
Collectibility	***
Parts/Service Availability	****
Est. Annual Maintenance Costs	$450

1981 Corvette Replacement Costs for Common Parts

Windshield (correct reproduction)	$450
Seat upholstery (pair, correct vinyl)	$250
Seat upholstery (pair, correct leather)	$390
Carpet	$200
Door panels (pair, correct reproduction w/out trim)	$210
Hood	$475
Front fender (correct press-molded reproduction)	$315
Wheel (cast aluminum)	$250
Headlamp assembly (including cup, ring, adjusters, bezel mount kit, and bulb)	$50
Taillamp lens	$55
Exhaust system (not including catalytic converter)	$275
Shock absorber	$75
Front wheel bearing	$15
Front springs (pair)	$100
Brake master cylinder (functional replacement)	$100
Brake caliper (stainless steel sleeved)	$100
Radiator (Harrison OEM type)	$475
Radiator support	$350
Water pump	$75 (rebuilt original)
Cylinder head (pair)	$200
Rear leaf spring (steel)	$110
Rear leaf spring (composite)	$310

1981 Corvette Specifications

Base price (new)	$16,258.52
Production	40,606
Engine	V-8
Bore x stroke (in inches)	4x3.48
Displacement	350-ci
Compression ratio	8.2:1 (base engine)
Horsepower	190 (base engine)
Transmission	4-speed manual or automatic standard
Wheelbase	98 inches
Overall width	69 inches
Overall height	47.7 inches
Overall length	185.3 inches
Track, front	58.7 inches
Track, rear	59.5 inches
Weight	3,282 pounds
Wheels	15x8 inches
Tires	P225/70R15 radials
Front suspension	independent unequal length wishbones and coil springs, anti-sway bar, telescopic shock absorbers
Rear suspension	independent radius arms, transverse leaf spring, anti-sway bar half shafts acting as upper locating members, lower transverse rods, telescopic shock absorbers
Steering	recirculating ball
Brakes	4-wheel disc, 4-piston calipers, 11.8-inch rotors front and rear
0 to 60 mph	7.2 seconds (350/190 w/ 2.87:1 axle and automatic transmission)
Standing 1/4[fraction font]-mile	15.4 seconds @ 91 mph (350/190 w/ 2.87:1 axle and automatic transmission)
Top speed	130 mph (350/190 w/ 2.87:1 axle and automatic transmission)

The chrome air cleaner lid brought a little bit of sparkle back into Corvette's engine compartment for 1981. For the first time since 1955, no optional engines were offered for Corvette.

If you intend to show your car at top-level events, such as those run by the National Corvette Restorers Society, or are simply a stickler for factory authenticity, do your best to seek out a car that is complete and unmolested under the hood. Restoring a basket case to look like this will take a lot more time and money than you think.

The interior for 1981 was almost indistinguishable from the previous year's. One hint that this is a 1981 is the ensemble of switches along the bottom of the seat. For the first time in Corvette history, a power driver-side seat was offered, and nearly three out of four buyers ordered it.

As was true to all C3 interiors, the fit, finish, and general materials for 1981s were not of high quality. Damage like tears, cracks, and other signs of wear and tear seem to occur with little provocation. Almost everything needed to restore the interior is readily available, but the costs for a comprehensive restoration add up quickly.

1981 Corvette Major Options

		Quantity	Price
AU3	Power door locks	36,322	$145
A42	Power driver seat	29,200	$183
CC1	Removable glass roof panels	20,095	$414
C49	Electro-Clear rear defogger	36,893	$119
D84	Custom 2-tone exterior paint	5,352	$399
DG7	Electric sport mirrors	13,567	$117
F51	Heavy-duty shock absorbers	1,128	$37
FE7	Gymkhana suspension	7,803	$57
G92	Performance-axle ratio	2,400	$20
K35	Cruise control	32,522	$155
M18	4-speed manual transmission	5,757	no charge
MX3	Turbo Hydra-Matic transmission	34,849	no charge
N90	Aluminum wheels	36,485	$428
QGQ	P225/70R15 blackwall radial tires	663	no charge
QGR	P225/70R15 white letter radial tires	21,939	$72
QXH	P255/60R15 white letter radial tires	18,004	$491.92
U58	AM-FM stereo radio	5,145	$95
U69	AM-FM radio	851	no charge
U75	Power antenna	32,903	$55
UL5	Radio delete (credit)	315	–$118
UM4	AM-FM stereo ETR radio w/ 8-track	8,262	$386
UM5	AM-FM stereo ETR radio w/ 8-track and CB	792	$712
UM6	AM-FM stereo ETR radio w/ cassette	22,892	$423
UN5	AM-FM stereo ETR radio w/ cassette and CB	2,349	$750
V54	Roof panel carrier	3,303	$135
YF5	California emissions	4,951	$46
ZN1	Trailer package	916	$110

What They Said in 1981

The best part of the current Vette is its effortless low-rpm responsiveness to the throttle. . . . Meantime, you've got all the standardized GM life-of-Riley appurtenances to keep you company when the squeaks, rattles, and lurches over bumpy roads begin to take their toll on your peace of mind. —*Car and Driver*, December 1981

I Bought a 1981 Corvette

I wanted a 1980, 1981, or 1982, because they are the most comfortable and modern of all sharks. As far as cosmetics go, my preference was for a 1982 Collector Edition, but I really wanted a four-speed, so that ruled out the 1982. The car I wound up buying is a 1981 four-speed, and what attracted me to it was the silver over dark blue two-tone paint, its high level of originality, and the four-speed. I did some detailing under the hood and cleaned off the mold that was growing on the interior from the car, the result of being used so rarely and stored in a damp garage. —Cliff Tundas

Raised white-letter Goodyear Eagle GT radials sized at P255/60R15 were extra-cost options. Aluminum wheels were also optional, with steel rally rims wearing chrome center caps and polished stainless trim rings standard.

Check the function of absolutely everything when evaluating a car for purchase, including headlights, brake lights, park lights, and turn signals. As is true for all C3s, 1981 headlight doors are powered by vacuum motors, and their semi-complicated vacuum systems are prone to leaks. The mechanical elements of the hideaway doors can also develop problems, most frequently from rust, excessive wear, or collision-induced damage.

When evaluating a prospective purchase, let the engine get up to a stable operating temperature, then check the operation of all gauges. Also determine if the radio and all HVAC functions work properly.

A handsome profile and balanced proportions give this decades-old design a timelessness that few cars achieve. Reasonable power and excellent chassis balance also make 1981s outstanding drivers.

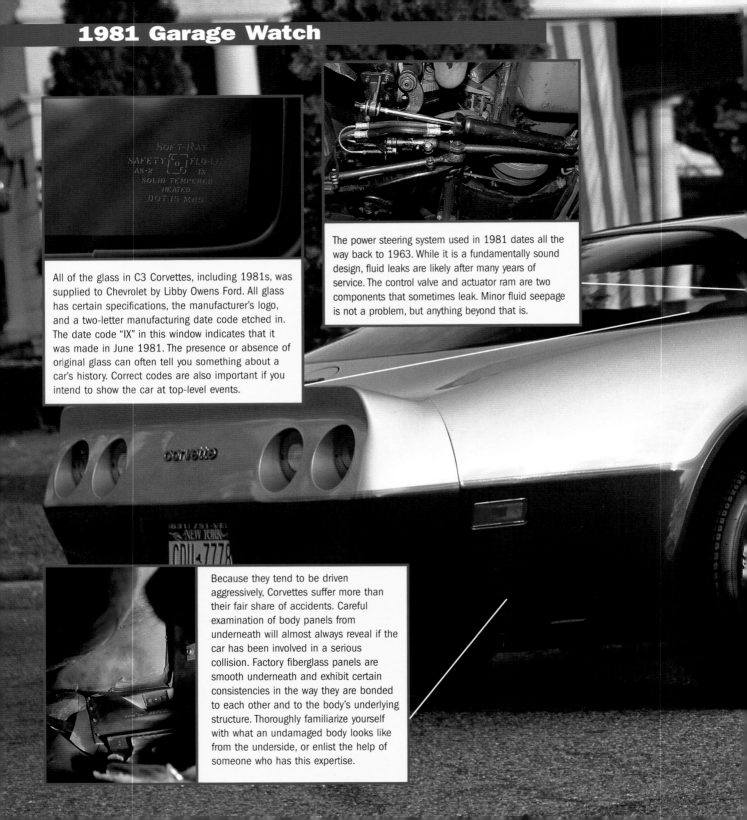

All of the glass in C3 Corvettes, including 1981s, was supplied to Chevrolet by Libby Owens Ford. All glass has certain specifications, the manufacturer's logo, and a two-letter manufacturing date code etched in. The date code "IX" in this window indicates that it was made in June 1981. The presence or absence of original glass can often tell you something about a car's history. Correct codes are also important if you intend to show the car at top-level events.

The power steering system used in 1981 dates all the way back to 1963. While it is a fundamentally sound design, fluid leaks are likely after many years of service. The control valve and actuator ram are two components that sometimes leak. Minor fluid seepage is not a problem, but anything beyond that is.

Because they tend to be driven aggressively, Corvettes suffer more than their fair share of accidents. Careful examination of body panels from underneath will almost always reveal if the car has been involved in a serious collision. Factory fiberglass panels are smooth underneath and exhibit certain consistencies in the way they are bonded to each other and to the body's underlying structure. Thoroughly familiarize yourself with what an undamaged body looks like from the underside, or enlist the help of someone who has this expertise.

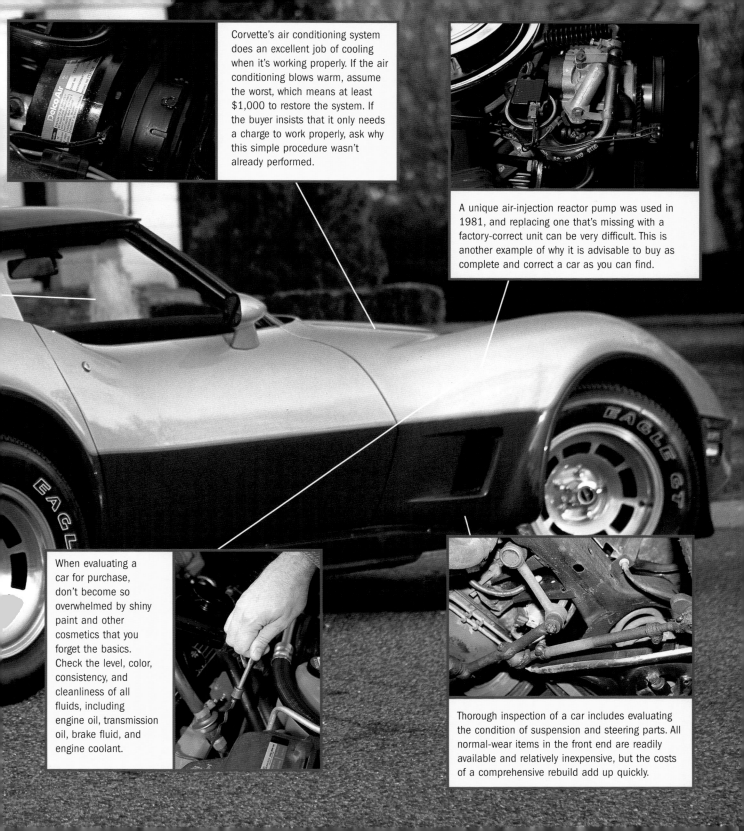

Corvette's air conditioning system does an excellent job of cooling when it's working properly. If the air conditioning blows warm, assume the worst, which means at least $1,000 to restore the system. If the buyer insists that it only needs a charge to work properly, ask why this simple procedure wasn't already performed.

A unique air-injection reactor pump was used in 1981, and replacing one that's missing with a factory-correct unit can be very difficult. This is another example of why it is advisable to buy as complete and correct a car as you can find.

When evaluating a car for purchase, don't become so overwhelmed by shiny paint and other cosmetics that you forget the basics. Check the level, color, consistency, and cleanliness of all fluids, including engine oil, transmission oil, brake fluid, and engine coolant.

Thorough inspection of a car includes evaluating the condition of suspension and steering parts. All normal-wear items in the front end are readily available and relatively inexpensive, but the costs of a comprehensive rebuild add up quickly.

Through 1981, C3s were built in Chevrolet's St. Louis, Missouri, assembly plant, Corvette's home since 1954. The transition to a modern plant in Bowling Green, Kentucky, was a major factor in elevating overall quality for 1982.

All 1982 Corvettes were built in Bowling Green, Kentucky, and overall build quality was perhaps the highest it had ever been to that point in Corvette's history. This was the last year for both the shark body style and original Sting Ray chassis design.

All 1982s were fitted with a 200-horsepower cross-fire injection 350. Cross-fire injection utilized two electronic carburetors that were directed by Chevrolet's Computer Command Control system for more precise metering of fuel. Though the same in principal to the system used in 1980 California-delivered cars and in all 1981s, Computer Command Control was significantly enhanced for 1982 with a much faster processor. It could make 80 adjustments per second, compared with the older version's 10 per second. Though scorned by some, especially those frustrated by the system's resistance to power enhancements, computer-directed cross-fire injection improved fuel economy, reduced emissions, and enhanced driveability.

For the first time since 1957, a four-speed manual transmission was not available in a Corvette. Fuel economy and emissions issues were mostly to blame for this sad development. A new four-speed automatic was the only transmission used.

By 1982, the Corvette was plenty long in the tooth and in dire need of some revitalization. The car's body design was in its fifteenth year, and its chassis layout dated all the way back to 1963. Everyone knew that an all-new Corvette would be introduced as a 1984 model, making it something of a challenge to keep the buying public focused on the 1982s. To that end, Chevrolet created a special Collector Edition hatchback.

Collector Editions featured distinct silver-beige paint with graduated contrasting graphics applied to the hood and sides. Bronze-tinted glass roof panels, unique cloisonné emblems, and finned, cast-aluminum wheels reminiscent of the optional cast aluminum bolt-ons offered in 1967 further distinguished the car's exterior appearance. Silver-beige leather upholstery, leather-wrapped steering wheel, leather-trimmed door panels, extra-plush carpeting, and a cloisonné emblem in the horn button carried the exterior theme to the inside.

A bit of added functionality was also given to the Collector Edition. The normally fixed large rear window, introduced with the fastback design in 1978, was made into a functioning hatch to allow easy access to the storage area beneath it.

Aside from the appearance changes, functional rear hatch, and inclusion of several otherwise optional features as standard, Collector Editions were the same as other 1982 models. That meant they were powered by the new Cross Fire Injection 350 and could only be had with automatic transmission. At $22,537.59, $4,247.52 more than a regular 1982, Collector Editions were not inexpensive for their day. Still, they were undeniably beautiful to many people, and an impressive total of 6,759 were ultimately built.

All 1982 Corvettes received a smaller, lighter catalytic converter and extensively revised exhaust pipes designed to retain heat. This change made the converter more efficient at catalyzing the oxidation of exhaust emissions. Also new for 1982 were an in-tank mounted electric fuel pump and a solenoid-operated inlet door in the hood that brought relatively cool outside air into the engine at full throttle.

Because they are the last of the series, far fewer were sold, and, undoubtedly, because they were the best built in many ways, 1982s are particularly attractive to many collectors. Because of this, you should expect to pay 10 to 20 percent more for a 1982 than you would for an otherwise comparable 1980 or 1981.

As with all C3s, 1982s are susceptible to rust in certain areas, including the chassis, windshield frame, radiator support, door housings, and trailing arms. Ever-increasing mechanical and electrical complexity, owing not only to the plethora of emissions reducing equipment found on 1982s and some earlier C3s, but also to the steady addition of more and more features, makes them more prone to certain problems. These include sensor, solenoid, and valve failures; vacuum leaks; electrical shorts; and catalytic converter failure.

Carefully evaluate the function of all systems and components when considering a car for purchase. Be sure to run and drive it at full operating temperature, which is when certain problems such as a bad positraction unit and a slipping transmission will more likely manifest themselves.

As is always the case, do your best to find and buy the highest quality car that you can afford. Paying more up front to obtain a car that needs little or nothing will save you a great deal of time and money down the road.

The silver and beige leather interior was unique to the 1982 Collector Edition, and replacement trim items are quite a bit more expensive than those for standard 1982 Corvettes.

1982 Corvette Ratings

Model Comfort/Amenities	*****
Reliability	****
Collectibility	****
Parts/Service Availability	****
Est. Annual Maintenance Costs	$450

1982 Corvette Replacement Costs for Common Parts

Windshield (correct reproduction)	$450
Seat upholstery (pair, correct vinyl)	$250
Seat upholstery (pair, correct leather)	$390
Carpet	$200
Door panels (pair, correct reproduction w/out trim)	$210
Hood	$475
Front fender (correct press-molded reproduction)	$315
Wheel (cast aluminum)	$250
Headlamp assembly (including cup, ring, adjusters, bezel mount kit, and bulb)	$50
Taillamp lens	$55
Exhaust system	$275
Shock absorber	$75
Front wheel bearing	$15
Front springs (pair)	$100
Brake master cylinder (functional replacement)	$100
Brake caliper (stainless steel sleeved)	$100
Radiator (Harrison OEM type)	$475
Radiator support	$350
Water pump	$75 (rebuilt original)
Cylinder head (pair)	$200
Rear leaf spring (composite)	$310

1982 Corvette Specifications

Base price (new)	$18,290.07 (Sport Coupe)
	$22,537.59 (Collector Edition hatchback)
Production	18,648 (Sport Coupe)
	6,759 (Collector Edition hatchback)
Engine	V-8
Bore x stroke (inches)	4x3.48
Displacement	350-ci
Compression ratio	8.2:1 (base engine)
Horsepower	200 (base engine)
Transmission	3-speed automatic
Wheelbase	98 inches
Overall width	69 inches
Overall height	47.7 inches
Overall length	184.7 inches
Track, front	58.7 inches
Track, rear	59.5 inches
Weight	3,585 pounds
Wheels	15x8 inches
Tires	P225/70R15 radials
Front suspension	independent unequal-length wishbones and coil springs, anti-sway bar, telescopic shock absorbers
Rear suspension	independent radius arms, transverse composite leaf spring, anti-sway bar half shafts acting as upper locating members, lower transverse rods, telescopic shock absorbers
Steering	recirculating ball
Brakes	4-wheel disc, 4-piston calipers, 11.8-inch rotors front and rear
0 to 60 mph	6.7 seconds (350/250 w/ 2.87:1 axle and automatic transmission)
Standing 1/4-mile	16.1 seconds @ 84.5 mph (350/200 w/ 2.87:1 axle and automatic transmission)
Top speed	125 mph (350/200 w/ 2.87:1 axle and automatic transmission)

Cross-fire injection was essentially comprised of two electronic carburetors controlled by the car's Computer Command Control system. It replaced the conventional carburetor used in 1981 and earlier. Cross-fire injection was used in 1982 and 1984 only, with a genuine fuel injection system called tuned-port introduced in 1985.

The 1982 Corvette engine compartment was perhaps the most crowded and complicated in Corvette history. The cross-fire injection air cleaner and induction setup were used in 1982 models only, making parts rather difficult to come by.

Despite better build quality than ever before, the 1982 interior was still just as prone to premature wear as other C3s. Upholstery on the sides bolsters is often damaged, and plastic trim throughout the interior breaks very easily. AM/FM stereo with cassette and CB radio was by far the most expensive option available in 1982.

A functional glass hatch was used exclusively with 1982 Collector Edition cars. It makes loading and unloading the rear storage area much easier. Struts that hold the hatch open can lose their effectiveness over time, however.

1982 Corvette Major Options

		Quantity	Price
AG9	Power driver seat	22,585	$197
AU3	Power door locks	23,936	$155
CC1	Removable glass roof panels	14,763	$443
C49	Electro-Clear rear defogger	16,886	$129
D84	Custom 2-tone exterior paint	4,871	$428
DG7	Electric sport mirrors	20,301	$125
FE7	Gymkhana suspension	5,457	$61
K35	Cruise control	24,313	$165
L83	350/200-horsepower engine	25,407	standard
MD8	Turbo Hydra-Matic transmission	25,407	no charge
N90	Aluminum wheel	16,844	$458
QGQ	P225/70R15 blackwall radial tires	405	no charge
QGR	P225/70R15 white letter radial tires	5,932	$80
QXH	P255/60R15 white letter radial tires	19,070	$542.52
U58	AM-FM stereo radio	1,533	$101
U75	Power antenna	15,557	$60
UL5	Radio delete (credit)	150	–$124
UM4	AM-FM stereo ETR radio w/ 8-track	923	$386
UM6	AM-FM stereo ETR radio w/ cassette	20,355	$423
UN5	AM-FM stereo ETR radio w/ cassette and CB	1,987	$755 ($695 w/ Collector Edition hatchback)
V08	Heavy-duty cooling	6,006	$57
V54	Roof panel carrier	1,992	$144
YF5	California emissions	4,951	$46

What They Said in 1982

Even though the TBI V-8 and Turbo Hydra-Matic powertrain will pull you to a higher terminal speed . . . it takes so long to get there you'll need Nebraska. The handling and braking offer more security than the good hands of Allstate. —*Car and Driver,* March 1982

I Bought a 1982 Corvette

I fell in love with the Collector Edition the moment I saw it and knew someday I would own one. I got it from the original owner, who bought it as an investment. It turned out to be not such a good investment, because Chevy sold a lot of them and most people took good care of theirs. I got mine with 5,400 miles, and after enjoying it for the past six years, I added another 9,000. The original tires were pretty hard, and since I wanted to save them anyway, I bought a new set of Goodyear Eagle radials. The only other thing I've done is change fluids. —Hector Sanchez

New leather seat covers for regular 1982 Corvettes cost about $390, and special Collector Edition covers cost a whopping $540. Add the cost of new foam and labor for the installation, and you quickly realize the value of paying more for a car that doesn't need seat covers or other interior items.

Examine the radiator support and surrounding components for signs of collision trauma. Bent parts, mount holes that had to be enlarged for the fastener to work, and a whole bunch of new parts in this area are all signs of trouble.

The unique cast-aluminum wheels on Collector Edition Corvettes were painted and trimmed to coordinate with the silver and beige paint scheme. Their styling is clearly reminiscent of the cast-aluminum bolt-on wheel option offered in 1967.

The Corvette Collector Edition hatchback was offered in 1982 to commemorate the end of the highly successful C3 body style. Despite being the most expensive Corvette to that point, Collector Editions constituted more than 25 percent of the year's production.

1982 Garage Watch

Cross-fire injection was designed to improve fuel economy and reduce emissions. Despite the fact that it generated decent power and was reasonably reliable, the system found little favor with enthusiasts, because it could not be readily modified for better performance.

Because they tend to be driven aggressively, Corvettes suffer more than their fair share of collision damage. Careful examination of the components behind the front-bumper cover often reveals whether a car was involved in a serious front-end collision.

It is essential to look underneath any car you are considering for purchase. Condition of the aluminum impact bar and related hardware behind the bumper cover can tell you whether the car was hit from behind. While you are examining the rear area, check to see if spare tire is present in the carrier, and take a look up at the gas tank to see if it is rusting.

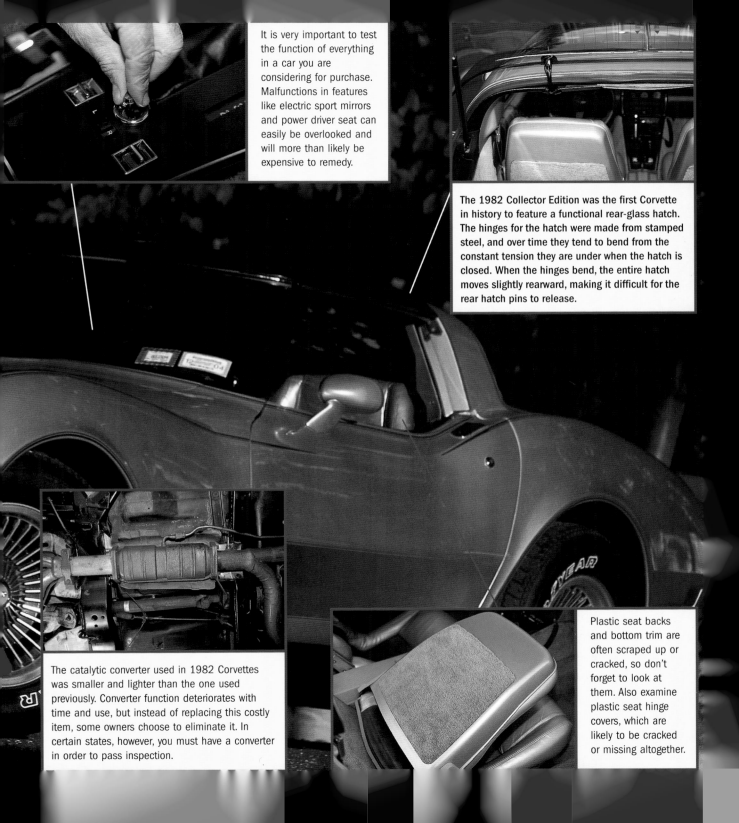

It is very important to test the function of everything in a car you are considering for purchase. Malfunctions in features like electric sport mirrors and power driver seat can easily be overlooked and will more than likely be expensive to remedy.

The 1982 Collector Edition was the first Corvette in history to feature a functional rear-glass hatch. The hinges for the hatch were made from stamped steel, and over time they tend to bend from the constant tension they are under when the hatch is closed. When the hinges bend, the entire hatch moves slightly rearward, making it difficult for the rear hatch pins to release.

The catalytic converter used in 1982 Corvettes was smaller and lighter than the one used previously. Converter function deteriorates with time and use, but instead of replacing this costly item, some owners choose to eliminate it. In certain states, however, you must have a converter in order to pass inspection.

Plastic seat backs and bottom trim are often scraped up or cracked, so don't forget to look at them. Also examine plastic seat hinge covers, which are likely to be cracked or missing altogether.

Appendix 1

Which C3 Do I Want?

Available Engines

Year	Designation	Cubic-Inch Displacement/ Horsepower
1968	Base	327/300
	L79	327/350
	L36	427/390
	L68	427/400
	L71	427/435
	L88	427/430
	L89	427/435
1969	Base	350/300
	L46	350/350
	L36	427/390
	L68	427/400
	L71	427/435
	L88	427/430
	L89	427/435
	ZL1	427/430
1970	Base	350/300
	L46	350/350
	LT1	350/370
	LS5	454/390
1971	Base	350/270
	LT1	350/330
	LS5	454/365
1972	Base	350/200
	LT1	350/255
	LS5	454/270
1973	Base L48	350/190
	L82	350/250
	LS4	454/275
1974	Base L48	350/195
	L82	350/250
	LS4	454/270
1975	Base L48	350/165
	L82	350/205
1976	Base L48	350/180
	L82	350/210
1977	Base L48	350/180
	L82	350/210
1978	Base L48	350/185
	L82	350/220
1979	Base L48	350/195
	L82	350/225
1980	Base L48	350/190
	L82	350/230
	LG4	305/180
1981	Base L81	350/190
1982	Base L83	350/200

Available Transmissions

Year	Transmission
1968	Base 3-speed manual
	M20 4-speed manual wide-ratio
	M21 4-speed manual close-ratio
	M22 4-speed manual close-ratio heavy-duty
	M40 3-speed automatic
1969	Base 3-speed manual
	M20 4-speed manual wide-ratio
	M21 4-speed manual close-ratio
	M22 4-speed manual close-ratio heavy-duty
	M40 3-speed automatic
1970	M20 4-speed manual wide-ratio
	M21 4-speed manual close-ratio
	M22 4-speed manual close-ratio heavy-duty
	M40 3-speed automatic
1971	M20 4-speed manual wide-ratio
	M21 4-speed manual close-ratio
	M22 4-speed manual close-ratio heavy-duty
	M40 3-speed automatic
1972	M20 4-speed manual wide-ratio
	M21 4-speed manual close-ratio
	M22 4-speed manual close-ratio heavy-duty
	M40 3-speed automatic
1973	M20 4-speed manual wide-ratio
	M21 4-speed manual close-ratio
	M40 3-speed automatic
1974	M20 4-speed manual wide-ratio
	M21 4-speed manual close-ratio
	M40 3-speed automatic
1975	M20 4-speed manual wide-ratio
	M21 4-speed manual close-ratio
	M40 3-speed automatic
1976	M20 4-speed manual wide-ratio
	M21 4-speed manual close-ratio
	M40 3-speed automatic
1977	M20 4-speed manual wide-ratio
	M21 4-speed manual close-ratio
	M40 3-speed automatic
1978	M20 4-speed manual wide-ratio
	M21 4-speed manual close-ratio
	M38 3-speed automatic
1979	M20 4-speed manual wide-ratio
	M21 4-speed manual close-ratio
	M38 3-speed automatic
1980	M20 4-speed manual wide-ratio
	M21 4-speed manual close-ratio
	M38 3-speed automatic
1981	M20 4-speed manual wide-ratio
	M21 4-speed manual close-ratio
	M38 3-speed automatic
1982	MD8 4-speed automatic

Appendix 2
C3 Numbers and Codes

Production Totals

Year	Production
1968	9,936 coupes, 18,630 convertibles, 28,566 total
1969	22,129 coupes, 16,633 convertibles, 38,762 total
1970	10,668 coupes, 6,648 convertibles, 17,316 total
1971	14,680 coupes, 7,121 convertibles, 21,801 total
1972	20,496 coupes, 6,508 convertibles, 27,004 total
1973	25,521 coupes, 4,943 convertibles, 30,464 total
1974	32,028 coupes, 5,474 convertibles, 37,502 total
1975	33,836 coupes, 4,629 convertibles, 38,465 total
1976	46,567 coupes
1977	49,213 coupes
1978	40,274 regular production coupes
1978	6,502 Indy 500 Pace Car replicas
1979	53,807 coupes
1980	40,614 coupes
1981	40,606 coupes
1982	18,648 regular production coupes
1982	6,759 Collector Editions

Vehicle Identification Numbers

Year	VIN Range
1968	194378S400001–194378S428566
1969	194379S700001–194379S738762
1970	194370S400001–194370S417316
1971	194371S100001–194371S121801
1972	1Z37K2S500001–1Z37K2S527004
1973	1Z37J3S400001–1Z37J3S434464
1974	1Z37J4S400001–1Z37J4S437502
1975	1Z37J5S400001–1Z37J5S438465
1976	1Z37L6S400001–1Z37L6S446558
1977	1Z37L7S400001–1Z37L7S449213
1978	1Z87L8S400001–1Z87L8S440274
1978	1Z87L8S900001–1Z87L8S906502 (Indy Pace Cars)
1979	1Z8789S400001–1Z8789S453807
1980	1Z878AS400001–1Z878AS440614
1981	1G1AY8764BS400001–1G1AY8764BS431611 (St. Louis, Missouri)
1981	1G1AY8764B5100001–1G1AY8764B5108995 (Bowling Green, Kentucky)
1982	1G1AY8786C5100001–1G1AY8786C5125407

1968–1971, the fourth character is a "6" for convertibles
1972–1975, the third character is a "6" for convertibles
1970–1980, the fifth character indicates what engine was originally installed into the car
1972, "K" indicates base engine, "L" indicates LT1, and "W" indicates 454
1973–1974, "J" indicates base engine, "T" indicates L82, and "Z" indicates 454
1975, "J" indicates base engine and "T" indicates L82
1976–1977, "L" indicates base engine and "X" indicates L82
1978, "L" indicates base engine and "4" indicates L82
1979, "8" indicates base engine and "4" indicates L82
1980, "8" indicates base engine, "L" indicates L82, and "H" indicates LG4 305-ci California engine

1968 C3 Engine Codes

HE	327/300 Base engine w/ Rochester Q-Jet, manual
HO	327/300 Base engine w/ Rochester Q-Jet, automatic
HP	327/300 Base engine w/ Rochester Q-Jet, a/c, p/s, manual
HT	327/350 L79 w/ Rochester Q-Jet, special camshaft, 4-speed
IL	427/390 L36 w/ Rochester Q-Jet, hydraulic lifters, 4-speed
IQ	427/390 L36 w/ Rochester Q-Jet, hydraulic lifters, automatic
IM	427/400 L68 w/ Holley 3x2 carburetors, hydraulic lifters, 4-speed
IO	427/400 L68 w/ Holley 3x2 carburetors, hydraulic lifters, automatic
IR	427/435 L71 w/ Holley 3x2 carburetors, mechanical lifters, 4-speed
IU	427/435 L89 w/ Holley 3x2 carburetors, mechanical lifters, aluminum cylinder heads, 4-speed
IT	427/430 L88 heavy-duty engine w/ Holley four-barrel, mechanical lifters, M22 4-speed

1969 C3 Engine Codes

HY	350/300 Base engine w/ Rochester Q-Jet, manual
HZ	350/300 Base engine w/ Rochester Q-Jet, automatic
HW	350/350 L46 w/ Rochester Q-Jet, special camshaft, 4-speed
HX	350/350 L46 w/ Rochester Q-Jet, special camshaft, a/c, 4-speed
GD	350/350 L46 w/ Rochester Q-Jet, special camshaft, a/c, K66, 4-speed
LM	427/390 L36 w/ Rochester Q-Jet, hydraulic lifters, four-speed
LL	427/390 L36 w/ Rochester Q-Jet, hydraulic lifters, automatic
LQ	427/400 L68 w/ Holley 3x2 carburetors, hydraulic lifters, 4-speed
LN	427/400 L68 w/ Holley 3x2 carburetors, hydraulic lifters, automatic
LO	427/430 L88 heavy-duty engine w/ Holley four-barrel, mechanical lifters, M22 4-speed
LV	427/430 L88 heavy-duty engine w/ Holley four-barrel, mechanical lifters, automatic
LR	427/435 L71 w/ Holley 3x2 carburetors, mechanical lifters, 4-speed
LX	427/435 L71 w/ Holley 3x2 carburetors, mechanical lifters, automatic
LP	427/435 L89 w/ Holley 3x2 carburetors, mechanical lifters, aluminum cylinder heads, 4-speed
LW	427/435 L89 w/ Holley 3x2 carburetors, mechanical lifters, aluminum cylinder heads, automatic
LT	427/435 L71 w/ Holley 3x2 carburetors, mechanical lifters, MA6, 4-speed
LU	427/435 L89 w/ Holley 3x2 carburetors, mechanical lifters, aluminum cylinder heads, MA6, 4-speed
ME	427/430 ZL1 performance package, aluminum block, heavy-duty engine w/ Holley four-barrel, mechanical lifters, M22
MG	427/430 ZL1 performance package, aluminum block, heavy-duty engine w/ Holley four-barrel, mechanical lifters, automatic
MH	427/390 L36 w/ Rochester Q-Jet, hydraulic lifters, K66, four-speed

1970 C3 Engine Codes

CTL	350/300 Base engine w/ Rochester Q-Jet, 4-speed (earlier base engine code)
CTD	350/300 Base engine w/ Rochester Q-Jet, 4-speed (later base engine code)
CTM	350/300 Base engine w/ Rochester Q-Jet, automatic (earlier base engine code)
CTG	350/300 Base engine w/ Rochester Q-Jet, automatic (later base engine code)
CTN	350/350 L46 w/ Rochester Q-Jet, special camshaft, 4-speed (earlier L46 code)
CTH	350/350 L46 w/ Rochester Q-Jet, special camshaft, 4-speed (later L46 code)
CTO	350/350 L46 w/ Rochester Q-Jet, special camshaft, a/c, 4-speed (earlier L46 code)
CTJ	350/350 L46 w/ Rochester Q-Jet, special camshaft, a/c, 4-speed (later L46 code)
CTP	350/350 L46 w/ Rochester Q-Jet, special camshaft, a/c, 4-speed
CTQ	350/350 L46 w/ Rochester Q-Jet, special camshaft, a/c, K66, 4-speed
CTU	350/370 LT1 w/ Holley four-barrel, mechanical lifters, K66, 4-speed (earlier LT1 code)
CTK	350/370 LT1 w/ Holley four-barrel, mechanical lifters, K66, 4-speed (later LT1 code)
CTV	350/370 ZR1 performance package, LT1 engine, M22
CZU	454/390 LS5 w/ Rochester Q-Jet, hydraulic lifters, four-speed
CGW	454/390 LS5 w/ Rochester Q-Jet, hydraulic lifters, automatic
CRI	454/390 LS5 w/ Rochester Q-Jet, hydraulic lifters, K66, four-speed
CRJ	454/390 LS5 w/ Rochester Q-Jet, hydraulic lifters, K66, automatic

1971 C3 Engine Codes

CJL	350/270	Base engine w/ Rochester Q-Jet, 4-speed
CGT	350/270	Base engine w/ Rochester Q-Jet, automatic (earlier base engine code)
CJK	350/270	Base engine w/ Rochester Q-Jet, automatic (later base engine code)
CGZ	350/330	LT1 w/ Holley four-barrel, mechanical lifters, 4-speed
CGY	350/330	ZR1 performance package, LT1 engine, M22
CPH	454/365	LS5 w/ Rochester Q-Jet, hydraulic lifters, four-speed
CPJ	454/365	LS5 w/ Rochester Q-Jet, hydraulic lifters, automatic
CPW	454/425	LS6 w/ Holley four-barrel, mechanical lifters, aluminum cylinder heads, M22 4-speed
CPX	454/425	LS6 w/ Holley four-barrel, mechanical lifters, aluminum cylinder heads, automatic

1972 C3 Engine Codes

CKW	350/200	Base engine w/ Rochester Q-Jet, 4-speed
CDH	350/200	Base engine w/ Rochester Q-Jet, NB2, 4-speed
CKX	350/200	Base engine w/ Rochester Q-Jet, automatic
CDJ	350/200	Base engine w/ Rochester Q-Jet, NB2, automatic
CKY	350/255	LT1 w/ Holley four-barrel, mechanical lifters, 4-speed
CRT	350/255	LT1 w/ Holley four-barrel, mechanical lifters, K19, 4-speed
CKZ	350/255	ZR1 performance package, LT1 engine, M22
CPH	454/270	LS5 w/ Rochester Q-Jet, hydraulic lifters, four-speed
CPJ	454/270	LS5 w/ Rochester Q-Jet, hydraulic lifters, automatic
CSR	454/270	LS5 w/ Rochester Q-Jet, hydraulic lifters, K19, four-speed
CSS	454/270	LS5 w/ Rochester Q-Jet, hydraulic lifters, K19, automatic

1973 C3 Engine Codes

CKZ	350/190	L48 w/ 4-speed
CLA	350/190	L48 engine w/ automatic
CLB	350/190	L48 engine w/ 4-speed (California)
CLC	350/190	L48 engine w/ automatic (California)
CLD	350/250	L82 w/ automatic
CLH	350/250	L82 engine w/ automatic (California)
CLR	350/250	L82 engine w/ 4-speed
CLS	350/250	L82 engine w/ 4-speed (California)
CWM	454/275	LS4 w/ 4-speed
CWR	454/275	LS4 w/ automatic
CWS	454/275	LS4 w/ automatic (California)
CWT	454/275	LS4 w/ 4-speed (California)

1974 C3 Engine Codes

CKZ	350/195	L48 w/ 4-speed
CLA	350/195	L48 engine w/ automatic
CLB	350/195	L48 engine w/ 4-speed (California)
CLC	350/195	L48 engine w/ automatic (California)
CLD	350/250	L82 w/ automatic (federal & some California)
CLH	350/250	L82 engine w/ automatic (California)
CLR	350/250	L82 engine w/ 4-speed (federal & some California)
CLS	350/250	L82 engine w/ 4-speed (federal)
CWM	454/270	LS4 w/ 4-speed (federal & some California)
CWR	454/270	LS4 w/ automatic
CWS	454/270	LS4 w/ automatic (California)
CWT	454/270	LS4 w/ 4-speed (California)

1975 C3 Engine Codes

CHA	350/165	L48 w/ 4-speed (federal)
CHB	350/165	L48 w/ automatic (federal)
CHC	350/205	L82 w/ 4-speed (federal)
CHR	350/205	L82 engine w/ automatic (federal & California)
CHU	350/165	L48 w/ 4-speed (federal)
CHZ	350/165	L48 w/ automatic (federal)
CKC	350/205	L82 engine w/ automatic (federal)
CRJ	350/165	L48 w/ 4-speed (federal)
CRK	350/165	L48 w/ automatic (federal)
CRL	350/205	L82 w/ 4-speed (federal)
CRM	350/205	L82 engine w/ automatic (federal)
CUA	350/165	L48 w/ 4-speed (federal)
CUB	350/165	L48 w/ automatic (federal)
CUD	350/205	L82 w/ 4-speed (federal)
CUT	350/205	L82 w/ 4-speed (federal)

1976 C3 Engine Codes

CHC	350/210	L82 w/ 4-speed (federal)
CKC	350/210	L82 engine w/ Turbo Hydra-Matic 400 (federal)
CKW	350/180	L48 w/ 4-speed (federal)
CKX	350/180	L48 engine w/ Turbo Hydra-Matic 350 (federal)
CLM	(Unverified usage)	
CLR	(Unverified usage)	
CLS	350/180	L48 engine w/ Turbo Hydra-Matic 350 (California)

1977 C3 Engine Codes

CHD	350/180	L48 w/ Turbo Hydra-Matic 350 (California)
CKD	350/180	L48 w/ Turbo Hydra-Matic 350 (high altitude)
CKZ	350/180	L48 w/ 4-speed (federal)
CLA	350/180	L48 engine w/ Turbo Hydra-Matic 350 (federal)
CLB	350/180	L48 w/ Turbo Hydra-Matic 350 (high altitude) (used in early production)
CLC	350/180	L48 w/ Turbo Hydra-Matic 350 (California) (used in early production)
CLD	350/210	L82 engine w/ 4-speed (federal)
CLF	350/210	L82 engine w/ Turbo Hydra-Matic 400 (federal)

1978 C3 Engine Codes

CHW	350/185	L48 w/ 4-speed (federal)
CLM	350/185	L48 w/ Turbo Hydra-Matic 350 (federal)
CLR	350/175	L48 w/ Turbo Hydra-Matic 350 (California)
CLS	350/175	L48 w/ Turbo Hydra-Matic 350 (high altitude)
CMR	350/220	L82 engine w/ 4-speed (federal)
CMS	350/220	L82 engine w/ Turbo Hydra-Matic 350 (federal)
CUT	350/185	L48 w/ Turbo Hydra-Matic 350 (federal)

1979 C3 Engine Codes

ZAA	350/195	L48 w/ 4-speed (federal) (early)
ZAB	350/195	L48 w/ Turbo Hydra-Matic 350 (federal) (early)
ZAC	350/195	L48 w/ Turbo Hydra-Matic 350 (California) (early)
ZAD	350/195	L48 w/ Turbo Hydra-Matic 350 (high altitude)
ZAF	350/195	L48 engine w/ 4-speed (federal)
ZAH	350/195	L48 w/ Turbo Hydra-Matic 350 (federal)
ZAJ	350/195	L48 w/ Turbo Hydra-Matic 350 (California)
ZBA	350/225	L82 engine w/ 4-speed (federal)
ZBB	350/225	L82 engine w/ Turbo Hydra-Matic 350 (federal)

1980 C3 Engine Codes

ZAK	350/190	L48 w/ Turbo Hydra-Matic 350 (federal)
ZAM	350/190	L48 w/ 4-speed (federal)
ZBC	350/230	L82 engine w/ Turbo Hydra-Matic 350 (federal)
ZBD	350/230	L82 engine w/ 4-speed (federal)
ZCA	305/180	LG4 w/ Turbo Hydra-Matic 350 (California)

1981 C3 Engine Codes

ZDA	350/190	L81 w/ 4-speed (federal)
ZDB	350/190	L81 w/ Turbo Hydra-Matic 350 (California)
ZDC	350/190	L81 engine w/ 4-speed (California)
ZDD	350/190	L81 w/ Turbo Hydra-Matic 350 (federal)

1982 C3 Engine Codes

ZBA	350/200	L83 engine w/ Turbo Hydra-Matic 700-R4 (federal)
ZBC	350/200	L83 w/ Turbo Hydra-Matic 700-R4 (California) (early)
ZBN	350/200	L83 w/ Turbo Hydra-Matic 700-R4 (California)

1968 Engine Block Casting Numbers

Casting Number	Description
3914460	early 327/300
3914678	327
3916321	early 427
3935439	late 427

1968 Engine Block Casting Numbers

Casting Number	Description
3932386	very early 350
3932388	possible 350 usage
3956618	midyear 350
3970010	late 350
3935439	early 427
3955270	early 427
3963512	late 427
3946052	ZL1 aluminum block

1970–1971 Engine Block Casting Numbers

Casting Number	Description
3970010	350
3963512	454

]1972–1974 Engine Block Casting Numbers

Casting Number	Description
3970010	350
3970014	late 1972 and early 1973 350
3999289	454

1975–1977 Engine Block Casting Numbers

Casting Number	Description
3970010	350

1978 Engine Block Casting Numbers

Casting Number	Description
3970010	350
376450	350
460703	350

1979 Engine Block Casting Numbers

Casting Number	Description
3970010	350
14016379	late 350

1980 Engine Block Casting Numbers

Casting Number	Description
3970010	350
14010207	350
4715111	LG4 California 305

1981–1982 Engine Block Casting Numbers

Casting Number	Description
14010207	350

1968 Body Build Date Codes

A	August 1967
B	September 1967
C	October 1967
D	November 1967
E	December 1967
F	January 1968
G	February 1968
H	March 1968
I	April 1968
J	May 1968
K	June 1968
L	July 1968
M	August 1968

1969 Body Build Date Codes

A	August 1968
B	September 1968
C	October 1968
D	November 1968
E	December 1968
F	January 1969
G	February 1969
H	March 1969
I	April 1969
J	May 1969
K	June 1969
L	July 1969
M	August 1969
N	September 1969
O	October 1969
P	November 1969
Q	December 1969

1970 Body Build Date Codes

A	January 1970
B	February 1970
C	March 1970
D	April 1970
E	May 1970
F	June 1970
G	July 1970

1971 Body Build Date Codes

A	August 1970
B	September 1970
C	October 1970
D	November 1970
E	December 1970
F	January 1971
G	February 1971
H	March 1971
I	April 1971
J	May 1971
K	June 1971
L	July 1971

1972 Body Build Date Codes

A	August 1971
B	September 1971
C	October 1971
D	November 1971
E	December 1971
F	January 1972
G	February 1972
H	March 1972
I	April 1972
J	May 1972
K	June 1972
L	July 1972

1973 Body Build Date Codes

A	August 1972
B	September 1972
C	October 1972
D	November 1972
E	December 1972
F	January 1973
G	February 1973
H	March 1973
I	April 1973
J	May 1973
K	June 1973
L	July 1973

1974 Body Build Date Codes

A	August 1973
B	September 1973
C	October 1973
D	November 1973
E	December 1973
F	January 1974
G	February 1974
H	March 1974
I	April 1974
J	May 1974
K	June 1974
L	July 1974
M	August 1974
N	September 1974

1975 Body Build Date Codes

A	October 1974
B	November 1974
C	December 1974
D	January 1975
E	February 1975
F	March 1975
G	April 1975
H	May 1975
I	June 1975
J	July 1975

1976 Body Build Date Codes

A	August 1975
B	September 1975
C	October 1975
D	November 1975
E	December 1975
F	January 1976
G	February 1976
H	March 1976
I	April 1976
J	May 1976
K	June 1976
L	July 1976
M	August 1976

1977 Body Build Date Codes

A	August 1976
B	September 1976
C	October 1976
D	November 1976
E	December 1976
F	January 1977
G	February 1977
H	March 1977
I	April 1977
J	May 1977
K	June 1977
L	July 1977
M	August 1977

1978 Body Build Date Codes

A	September 1977
B	October 1977
C	November 1977
D	December 1977
E	January 1978
F	February 1978
G	March 1978
H	April 1978
I	May 1978
J	June 1978
K	July 1978
L	August 1978

1979 Body Build Date Codes

A	August 1978
B	September 1978
C	October 1978
D	November 1978
E	December 1978
F	January 1979
G	February 1979
H	March 1979
I	April 1979
J	May 1979
K	June 1979
L	July 1979
M	August 1979
N	September 1979

1980 Body Build Date Codes

A	October 1979
B	November 1979
C	December 1979
D	January 1980
E	February 1980
F	March 1980
G	April 1980
H	May 1980
I	June 1980
J	July 1980
K	August 1980

1981 Body Build Date Codes (Cars Assembled in St. Louis, Missouri)

A	August 1980
B	September 1980
C	October 1980
D	November 1980
E	December 1980
F	January 1981
G	February 1981
H	March 1981
I	April 1981
J	May 1981
K	June 1981
L	July 1981

1981 Body Build Date Codes (Cars Assembled in Bowling Green, Kentucky)

B05	May 1981
B06	June 1981
B07	July 1981
B08	August 1981
B09	September 1981
B10	October 1981

1982 Body Build Date Codes

C10	October 1981
C11	November 1981
C12	December 1981
C01	January 1982
C02	February 1982
C03	March 1982
C04	April 1982
C05	May 1982
C06	June 1982
C07	July 1982
C08	August 1982
C09	September 1982
C10	October 1982

1968 Trim Codes/Interior Color

STD	Black vinyl
402	Black leather
407	Red vinyl
408	Red leather
414	Medium Blue vinyl
415	Medium Blue leather
411	Dark Blue vinyl
425	Dark Orange vinyl
426	Dark Orange leather
435	Tobacco vinyl
436	Tobacco leather
442	Gunmetal vinyl

1968 Exterior Color Codes and Available Trim Combinations

900	Tuxedo Black (available w/ all interior colors)
421	Polar White (available w/ all interior colors)
974	Rally Red (STD, 402, 407, 408)
415	LeMans Blue (STD, 402, 414, 415, 411)
978	International Blue (STD, 402, 414, 415, 411)
983	British Green (STD, 402)
984	Safari Yellow (STD, 402)
52	Silverstone Silver (STD, 402, 442)
988	Cordovan Maroon (STD, 402)
26	Corvette Bronze (STD, 402, 425, 426, 435, 436)

1969 Trim Codes/Interior Color

STD	Black vinyl
ZQ4	Black vinyl
402	Black leather
407	Red vinyl
408	Red leather
411	Bright Blue vinyl, Bright Blue leather
427	Green vinyl
428	Green leather
420	Saddle vinyl
421	Saddle leather
416	Gunmetal vinyl
417	Gunmetal leather

1969 Exterior Color Codes and Available Trim Combinations

900	Tuxedo Black (available w/ all interior colors)
422	Can-Am White (available w/ all interior colors)
974	Monza Red (STD, ZQ4, 402, 407, 408, 420, 421)
976	LeMans Blue (STD, ZQ4, 402, 411, 412)
980	Riverside Gold (STD, ZQ4, 402, 420, 421)
983	Fathom Green (STD, ZQ4, 402, 427, 428, 420, 421)
984	Daytona Yellow (STD, ZQ4, 402)
986	Cortez Silver (available with all interior colors)
988	Burgundy (STD, ZQ4, 402, 420, 421)
990	Monaco Orange (STD, ZQ4, 402)

1970 Trim Codes/Interior Color

400   Black vinyl
403   Black leather
407   Red vinyl
411   Blue vinyl
422   Green vinyl
418   Saddle vinyl
424   Saddle leather
414   Brown vinyl

1970 Exterior Color Codes and Available Trim Combinations

972   Classic White (available w/ all interior colors)
974   Monza Red (400, 403, 407, 418, 424, 414)
423   Marlboro Maroon (400, 403, 418, 424, 414)
976   Mulsanne Blue (400, 403, 411)
979   Bridgehampton Blue (400, 403, 411)
982   Donnybrooke Green (400, 402, 422, 418, 424, 414)
984   Daytona Yellow (400, 403, 422)
986   Cortez Silver (available w/ all interior colors)
992   Laguna Gray (available w/ all interior colors)
        Corvette Bronze (400, 403)

1971 Trim Codes/Interior Color

400   Black vinyl
403   Black leather
407   Red vinyl
412   Dark Blue vinyl
423   Dark Green vinyl
417   Saddle vinyl
420   Saddle leather

1971 Exterior Color Codes and Available Trim Combinations

905   Nevada Silver (400, 403, 407, 412, 423)
912   Sunflower Yellow (400, 403, 423, 417, 420)
972   Classic White (available w/ all interior colors)
973   Mille Miglia Red (400, 403, 407)
976   Mulsanne Blue (400, 403, 412)
979   Bridgehampton Blue (400, 403, 412)
983   Brands Hatch Green (400, 403, 423)
987   Ontario Orange (400, 403, 423, 417, 420)
988   Steel Cities Gray (400, 403, 417, 420)
13   War Bonnet Yellow (400, 403, 423, 417, 420)

1972 Trim Codes/Interior Color

400   Black vinyl
404   Black leather
407   Red vinyl
412   Blue vinyl
417   Saddle vinyl
421   Saddle leather

1972 Exterior Color Codes and Available Trim Combinations

924   Pewter Silver (available w/ all interior colors)
912   Sunflower Yellow (400, 404, 417, 421)
972   Classic White (available w/ all interior colors)
973   Mille Miglia Red (400, 404, 407, 417, 421)
945   Bryar Blue (400, 404)
979   Targa Blue (400, 404, 412)
946   Elkhart Green (400, 404, 421, 417)
987   Ontario Orange (400, 404, 417, 421)
988   Steel Cities Gray (400, 404, 407, 417, 421)
76   War Bonnet Yellow (400, 404, 417, 420)

1973 Trim Codes/Interior Color

400   Black vinyl
404   Black leather
425   Dark Red vinyl
413   Dark Blue vinyl
415   Medium Saddle vinyl
416   Medium Saddle leather
418   Dark Saddle vinyl
422   Dark Saddle leather

1973 Exterior Color Codes and Available Trim Combinations

910   Classic White (available w/ all interior colors)
914   Silver Metallic (available w/ all interior colors)
976   Mille Miglia Red (available w/ all interior colors)
922   Medium Blue Metallic (400, 404, 413, 415, 416)
927   Dark Blue Metallic (400, 404, 413, 415, 416, 425)
947   Elkhart Green Metallic (400, 404, 415, 416)
980   Orange Metallic (400, 404, 413, 415, 416, 418, 422)
953   Yellow Metallic (400, 404, 413)
952   Bright Yellow (400, 404, 413, 418, 422)
945   Blue-Green Metallic (400, 404, 415, 416, 418, 422, 425)

1974 Trim Codes/Interior Color

400   Black vinyl
404   Black leather
425   Dark Red vinyl
413   Dark Blue vinyl
415   Medium Saddle vinyl
416   Medium Saddle leather
406   Silver vinyl
407   Silver leather
408   Neutral vinyl

1974 Exterior Color Codes and Available Trim Combinations

910   Classic White (available with all interior colors)
914   Silver Mist Metallic (400, 404, 406, 407, 413, 415, 416, 425)
976   Mille Miglia Red (400, 404, 406, 407, 408, 415, 416, 425)
922   Medium Blue Metallic (400, 404, 406, 407, 413)
948   Dark Green Metallic (400, 404, 406, 407, 408, 415, 416)
980   Orange Metallic (400, 404, 406, 407, 408, 415, 416)
956   Bright Yellow (400, 404, 406, 407, 408, 415, 416)
968   Dark Brown Metallic (400, 404, 406, 407, 408, 415, 416)
917   Corvette Gray Metallic (available with all interior colors)
974   Medium Red Metallic (400, 404, 406, 407, 408, 415, 416, 425)

1975 Trim Codes/Interior Color

19V   Black vinyl
192   Black leather
73V   Dark Red vinyl
732   Dark Red leather
26V   Dark Blue vinyl
262   Dark Blue leather
65V   Medium Saddle vinyl
652   Medium Saddle leather
14V   Silver vinyl
142   Silver leather
60V   Neutral vinyl

1975 Exterior Color Codes and Available Trim Combinations

10   Classic White (available w/ all interior colors)
13   Silver Metallic (19V, 192, 73V, 732, 26V, 262, 65V, 652, 14V, 142)
76   Mille Miglia Red (19V, 192, 73V, 732, 60V, 65V, 652, 14V, 142)
22   Bright Blue Metallic (19V, 192, 26V, 262, 14V, 142)
27   Steel Blue Metallic (19V, 192, 26V, 262, 14V, 142)
42   Bright Green Metallic (19V, 192, 65V, 652, 14V, 142, 60V)
70   Orange Flame (19V, 192, 65V, 652, 60V)
56   Bright Yellow (19V, 192, 65V, 652, 60V)
67   Medium Saddle Metallic (19V, 192, 65V, 652, 60V)
74   Dark Red Metallic (19V, 192, 65V, 652, 14V, 142, 60V, 73V, 732)

1976 Trim Codes/Interior Color

19V   Black vinyl
192   Black leather
71V   Dark Firethorn vinyl
712   Dark Firethorn leather
322   Blue-Green leather
152   Smoke-Gray leather
64V   Light Buckskin vinyl
642   Light Buckskin leather
15V   White vinyl
112   White leather
692   Dark Brown leather

1976 Exterior Color Codes and Available Trim Combinations

10	Classic White (available w/ all interior colors)
13	Silver Metallic (19V, 192, 71V, 712, 322, 15V, 112, 152, 64V, 642)
72	Corvette Red (19V, 192, 71V, 712, 64V, 642, 15V, 112, 152)
22	Bright Blue Metallic (19V, 192, 152)
33	Dark Green Metallic (19V, 192, 64V, 642, 15V, 112, 152, 322)
70	Orange Flame (19V, 192, 64V, 642, 692)
56	Bright Yellow (19V, 192, 692)
64	Light Buckskin (15V, 112, 19V, 192, 64V, 642, 692, 71V, 712)
69	Dark Brown Metallic (19V, 192, 64V, 642, 15V, 112, 692)
37	Mahogany Metallic (19V, 192, 71V, 712, 15V, 112, 152, 64V, 642)

1977 Trim Codes/Interior Color

19C	Black cloth
192	Black leather
72C	Medium Red cloth
722	Medium Red leather
15C	Smoke-Gray cloth
152	Smoke-Gray leather
64C	Buckskin cloth
642	Buckskin leather
112	White leather
27C	Dark Blue cloth
272	Dark Blue leather
69C	Dark Brown cloth
692	Dark Brown leather

1977 Exterior Color Codes and Available Trim Combinations

10	Classic White (available w/ all interior colors)
13	Silver Metallic (19C, 192, 72C, 722, 27C, 272, 15C, 152)
19	Black (112, 19C, 192, 72V, 722, 64C, 642, 15C, 152)
26	Light Blue Metallic (112, 19C, 192, 15C, 152)
28	Dark Blue (112, 19C, 192, 15C, 152, 27C, 272, 64C, 642)
41	Chartreuse (19C, 192)
66	Orange Metallic (19C, 192, 64C, 642, 69C, 692)
52	Corvette Yellow (19C, 192, 69C, 692)(code # changed from 52 to 56 midyear)
80	Tan Buckskin (112, 19C, 192, 64C, 642, 69C, 692, 72C, 722)
83	Dark Red (19C, 192, 64C, 642, 15C, 152)
72	Medium Red (112, 19C, 192, 72C, 722, 15C, 152, 64C, 642)

1978 Trim Codes/Interior Color

15C	Silver cloth (Pace Car replica only)
152	Silver leather (Pace Car replica only)
19C	Black cloth
192	Black leather
72C	Medium Red cloth
722	Medium Red leather
76C	Saffron cloth
762	Saffron leather
59C	Light Doeskin cloth
592	Light Doeskin leather
12C	Oyster White cloth
122	Oyster White leather
29C	Dark Blue cloth
292	Dark Blue leather
69C	Dark Brown cloth
692	Dark Brown leather

1978 Exterior Color Codes and Available Trim Combinations

10	Classic White (available w/ all interior colors)
13	Silver Metallic (12C, 122, 19C, 192, 72C, 722, 29C, 292, 76C, 762)
19	Black (12C, 122, 19C, 192, 72C, 722, 59C, 592, 76C, 762)
52	Yellow (19C, 192, 69C, 692, 12C, 122)
59	Frost Beige (19C, 192, 72C, 722, 29C, 292, 76C, 762, 59C, 592, 69C, 692)
72	Red (19C, 192, 72V, 72C, 59C, 592, 12C, 122)
83	Dark Blue Metallic (122, 12C, 19C, 192, 72C, 722, 59C, 592, 29C, 292)
66	Orange Metallic (19C, 192, 64C, 642, 69C, 692)
82	Mahogany Metallic (122, 12C, 19C, 192, 76C, 762, 59C, 592)
	Dark Brown Metallic (122, 12C, 19C, 192, 59C, 592, 69C, 692)
13U/07M	Silver Anniversary (12C, 122, 19C, 192, 72C, 722, 29C, 292, 76C, 762)
19U/47M	Pace Car Replica (15C, 152)

1979 Trim Codes/Interior Color

192	Black leather
722	Medium Red leather
59C	Light Doeskin cloth
592	Light Doeskin leather
12C	Oyster White cloth
122	Oyster White leather
29C	Dark Blue cloth
292	Dark Blue leather
49C	Dark Green cloth
492	Dark Green leather

1979 Exterior Color Codes and Available Trim Combinations

10	Classic White (available w/ all interior colors)
13	Silver Metallic (12C, 122, 192, 722, 29C, 292, 49C, 492)
19	Black (12C, 122, 192, 722, 59C, 592)
28	Frost Blue (192, 29C, 292, 12C, 122)
52	Yellow (192, 59C, 592, 12C, 122)
58	Dark Green Metallic (192, 59C, 592, 49C, 492, 12C, 122)
59	Frost Beige (192, 722, 29C, 292, 49C, 492, 59C, 592)
68	Hilton Brown Metallic (192, 59C, 592, 12C, 122) (also appears as code 82)
72	Red (192, 722, 59C, 592, 12C, 122)
83	Dark Blue Metallic (122, 12C, 192, 722, 59C, 592, 29C, 292)

1980 Trim Codes/Interior Color

192	Black leather
722	Medium Red leather
59C	Light Doeskin cloth
592	Light Doeskin leather
12C	Oyster White cloth
122	Oyster White leather
29C	Dark Blue cloth
292	Dark Blue leather
492	Dark Green leather
79C	Claret cloth
792	Claret leather

1980 Exterior Color Codes and Available Trim Combinations

10	Classic White (available w/ all interior colors)
13	Silver Metallic (12C, 122, 192, 722, 29C, 292, 79C, 792, 492)
19	Black (12C, 122, 192, 722, 59C, 592)
28	Dark Blue Metallic (192, 722, 59C, 592, 29C, 292, 12C, 122)
52	Yellow (192, 12C, 122)
58	Dark Green Metallic (192, 59C, 592, 492, 12C, 122)
59	Frost Beige (192, 122, 12C, 29C, 292)
47	Hilton Brown Metallic (available w/ all interior colors)
83	Medium Red (192, 722, 59C, 592, 12C, 122)
76	Dark Claret Metallic (122, 12C, 192, 59C, 592, 79C, 792)

1981 Trim Codes/Interior Color

19C	Charcoal cloth

192	Charcoal leather
722	Medium Red leather
64C	Camel cloth
642	Camel leather
29C	Dark Blue cloth
292	Dark Blue leather
152	Silver leather
67C	Medium Cinnabar cloth
672	Medium Cinnabar leather

1981 Exterior Color Codes and Available Trim Combinations

06	Mahogany Metallic (64C, 642, 67C, 672)
10	Classic White (19C, 192, 722, 64C, 642, 29C, 292, 67C, 672)
13	Silver Metallic (19C, 192, 722, 152, 29C, 292)
19	Black (19C, 192, 722, 64C, 642, 152, 67C, 672)
24	Bright Blue Metallic (19C, 192, 152, 64C, 642, 29C, 292)
28	Dark Blue Metallic (722, 64C, 642, 29C, 292, 152)
52	Yellow (19C, 192, 64C, 642)
59	Frost Beige (722, 64C, 642, 29C, 292, 67C, 672)
75	Red (19C, 192, 722, 64C, 642, 152)
79	Maroon Metallic (19C, 192, 722, 64C, 642, 152)
84	Charcoal Metallic (19C, 192, 722, 64C, 642, 152)
33/38	Silver/Dark Blue (29C, 292, 152)
33/39	Silver/Charcoal (19C, 192, 152, 67C, 672)
50/74	Beige/Dark Bronze (64C, 642)
80/98	Red/Dark Claret (64C, 642, 152, 67C, 672)

1982 Trim Codes/Interior Color

592	Collector Edition Hatchback Silver Beige leather
132	Silver Gray leather
182	Charcoal leather
74C	Dark Red cloth
742	Dark Red leather
64C	Camel cloth
642	Camel leather
22C	Dark Blue cloth
222	Dark Blue leather
402	Silver Green leather

1982 Exterior Color Codes and Available Trim Combinations

10	Classic White (available w/ all interior colors)
13	Silver Metallic (132, 182, 74C, 742, 22C, 222)
19	Black (132, 182, 74C, 742, 64C, 642, 402)
24	Silver Blue Metallic (132, 182, 64C, 642)
26	Dark Blue Metallic (132, 64C, 642, 22C, 222)
31	Bright Blue Metallic (132, 182, 64C, 642, 22C, 222)
39	Charcoal Metallic (132, 182, 74C, 742)
40	Silver Green Metallic (182, 402)
56	Gold Metallic (132, 64C, 642)
59	Silver Beige Metallic (592)
70	Red (132, 182, 74C, 742, 64C, 642)
99	Dark Claret Metallic (132, 74C, 742, 64C, 642)
13/99	Silver/Dark Claret (132, 74C, 742)
24/26	Silver Blue/Dark Blue (22C, 222)
13/39	Silver/Charcoal (132, 182)
10/13	White/Silver (132, 182)

1968 Final Monthly Serial Numbers

September 1967	400905
October 1967	403410
November 1967	405682
December 1967	407922
January 1968	410386
February 1968	412647
March 1968	415000
April 1968	417676
May 1968	420928
June 1968	423978
July 1968	unknown
August 1968	428566

1969 Final Monthly Serial Numbers

September 1968	703041
October 1968	706272
November 1968	709159
December 1968	711742
January 1969	714695
February 1969	717571
March 1969	720543
April 1969	721315
May 1969	no cars built
June 1969	723374
July 1969	725875
August 1969	728107
September 1969	730963
October 1969	734067
November 1969	736798
December 1969	738762

1970 Final Monthly Serial Numbers

January 1970	402261
February 1970	405183
March 1970	407977
April 1970	408314
May 1970	410652
June 1970	413829
July 1970	417316

1971 Final Monthly Serial Numbers

August 1970	101212
September 1970	102226
October 1970	no cars built
November 1970	102675
December 1970	105269
January 1971	108230
February 1971	110886
March 1971	113626
April 1971	115983
May 1971	118223
June 1971	120686
July 1971	121801

[H]1972 Final Monthly Serial Numbers

August 1971	501344
September 1971	503697
October 1971	506050
November 1971	508406
December 1971	510310
January 1972	512661
February 1972	515020
March 1972	517613
April 1972	519993
May 1972	522611
June 1972	525226
July 1972	527004

1973 Final Monthly Serial Numbers

August 1972	401138
September 1972	403539
October 1972	406054
November 1972	408696
December 1972	410679
January 1973	413600
February 1973	416301
March 1973	419253
April 1973	421933
May 1973*	428892
June 1973	431731
July 1973	434464

*The May 1973 production total includes 4,000 serial numbers from 424001 through 428000 that were not utilized.

1974 Final Monthly Serial Numbers

August 1973	401250
September 1973	404111
October 1973	407605
November 1973	410813
December 1973	412830
January 1974	416184
February 1974	419258
March 1974	422367
April 1974	425751
May 1974	429602
June 1974	433257
July 1974	no cars built
August 1974	no cars built
September 1974	437502

[H]1975 Final Monthly Serial Numbers

October 1974	402385
November 1974	406180
December 1974	409110
January 1975	413159
February 1975	417112
March 1975	420856
April 1975	425228
May 1975	429379
June 1975	433474
July 1975	438465

1976 Final Monthly Serial Numbers

August 1975	401602
September 1975	405693
October 1975	409982
November 1975	413481
December 1975	416696
January 1976	420568
February 1976	424370
March 1976	428760
April 1976	432805
May 1976	436656
June 1976	440830
July 1976	444767
August 1976	446558

1977 Final Monthly Serial Numbers

August 1976	402287
September 1976	406337
October 1976	410547
November 1976	414216
December 1976	417551
January 1977	421118
February 1977	424662
March 1977	429041
April 1977	433057
May 1977	437029
June 1977	441233
July 1977	445179
August 1977	449213

1978 Final Monthly Serial Numbers

September 1977	403186
October 1977	407401
November 1977	411316
December 1977	414695
January 1978	418154
February 1978	422503
March 1978	425280
April 1978	no cars built
May 1978	428833
June 1978	433131
July 1978	436848
August 1978	440274

1978 Indy 500 Pace Car Replica Production

March 1978	901675
April 1978	905766
May 1978	906502

1979 Final Monthly Serial Numbers

August 1978	400770
September 1978	404612
October 1978	409292
November 1978	413389
December 1978	416891
January 1979	421182
February 1979	425115
March 1979	429500
April 1979	433259
May 1979	437626
June 1979	441770
July 1979	445884
August 1979	450434
September 1979	453807

1980 Final Monthly Serial Numbers

September 1979	400011
October 1979	404267
November 1979	408343
December 1979	411652
January 1980	416198
February 1980	420057
March 1980	424380
April 1980	427800
May 1980	431152
June 1980	434509
July 1980	438049
August 1980	440614

1981 St. Louis Assembled

August 1980	400775
September 1980	404136
October 1980	408594
November 1980	412124
December 1980	415234
January 1981	418399
February 1981	421392
March 1981	424742
April 1981	426422
May 1981	428003
June 1981	429775
July 1981	431611

1981 Bowling Green Assembled

June 1981	100692
July 1981	103155
August 1981	105025
September 1981	106896
October 1981	108995

1982* Final Monthly Serial Numbers

October 1981	100515
November 1981	100590
December 1981	102647
January 1982	105004
February 1982	107287
March 1982	110060
April 1982	112598
May 1982	115020
June 1982	117686
July 1982	120227
August 1982	121889
September 1982	124433
October 1982	125408

*Though the final serial number is 25,408, actual 1982 production totaled 25,407. The discrepancy is attributed to the loss of one serial number.

Appendix 3

Resources

Corvette Clubs

National Corvette Restorers Society
6291 Day Road
Cincinnati, OH 45252-1334
513-385-8526
www.ncrs.org

National Council of Corvette Clubs
Gail Dawley, VP of Membership
327 Baywood Drive
Campobello, SC 29322-9049
www.corvettenccc.org

Corvette Parts Sources

Zip Products
8067 Fast Lane
Mechanicsville, VA 23111
800-962-9632
www.zip-corvette.com

Mid America Direct
P.O. Box 1368
Effingham, IL 62401
800-500-8388
www.madvet.com

Corvette Central
P.O. Box 16
Sawyer, MI 49125
269-426-3342
www.corvettecentral.com

Paragon Reproductions
8040 South Jennings Rd.
Swartz Creek, MI 48473
800-882-4688
www.corvette-paragon.com

West Coast Corvettes
1031 S. Melrose Avenue
Placentia, CA 92870
888-737-8388
www.westcoastcorvette.com

Van Steel
12285 West Street
Clearwater, FL 33762
800-418-5397
www.vansteel.com

Not Just Vettes
904 Long Island Avenue
Deer Park, NY 11729
631-243-3333
www.partsforvettes.com

Corvette Dealers

Unique Corvettes
226 Belle Mead Rd
Setauket, New York 11733
631-751-8388
www.uniquecorvettes.com

Corvette Mike
1133 North Tustin Avenue
Anaheim, California 92807
800-327-8388
www.corvettemike.com

Pro Team Corvette Sales
P.O. Box 606
Napoleon, Ohio, 43545
888-592-5086
www.proteam-corvette.com

Magazines

Corvette Magazine
P.O. Box 1529
Ross, CA 94957
415-382-0580

Corvette Quarterly
Corvette Quarterly Subscription Center
P.O. Box 2063
Warren, MI 48090-2063
587-753-8338

Index

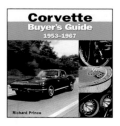
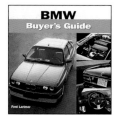
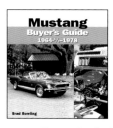

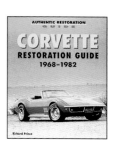